AMERICAN RESTORATION STYLE

BUNGALOW

AMERICAN RESTORATION STYLE

BUNGALOW

JAN CIGLIANO ▪▪▪ PHOTOGRAPHS BY WALTER SMALLING JR.

SALT LAKE CITY

First edition
02 01 00 99 98   5 4 3 2 1

Published by
Gibbs Smith, Publisher
P.O. Box 667
Layton, Utah 84041
Orders: (800) 748-5439
Visit our web site at www.gibbs-smith.com

Book design by Traci O'Very Covey

Printed and bound by Codra Enterprises, Inc. (Carson, CA) in Korea

Library of Congress Cataloging-in-Publication Data
Cigliano, Jan.
        Bungalow : American Restoration style / Jan Cigliano ;
photographs by Walter Smalling Jr. — 1st ed.
            p.   cm.
        Includes bibliographical references.
        ISBN 0-87905-852-8
        1. Bungalows—United States—Conservation and restoration.
    I. Title.
    NA7571.C54 1998
    728'.373'0973—dc21   98-13420
                                                      CIP

CONTENTS

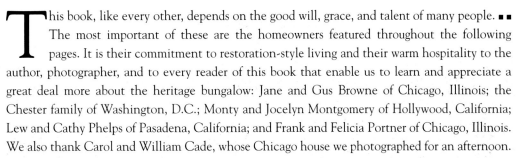

ACKNOWLEDGMENTS

This book, like every other, depends on the good will, grace, and talent of many people. ■ ■ The most important of these are the homeowners featured throughout the following pages. It is their commitment to restoration-style living and their warm hospitality to the author, photographer, and to every reader of this book that enable us to learn and appreciate a great deal more about the heritage bungalow: Jane and Gus Browne of Chicago, Illinois; the Chester family of Washington, D.C.; Monty and Jocelyn Montgomery of Hollywood, California; Lew and Cathy Phelps of Pasadena, California; and Frank and Felicia Portner of Chicago, Illinois. We also thank Carol and William Cade, whose Chicago house we photographed for an afternoon.

We thank the knowledgeable individuals who helped us research and scout houses and homeowners in each of the cities. In Chicago, Bill and Christine Cigliano (Jan's brother and sister-in-law) made the initial contacts and gave us a home-away-from-home; we are also indebted to Alice Sinkevitch of AIA Chicago, Darcie A. Wadycki of the Villa historic district, Peggy Zack of Oak Park, and Tim Barton of the Illinois Landmarks Commission. In Los Angeles, Linda Dishman and Christy McAvoy of the Los Angeles Conservancy identified houses and individuals. In Washington, D.C., we are indebted to Ben Van Dusen of Van Dusen Architects, who identified the Chester house; and to Jim Pandula of Blackburn Architects (the Chesters' restoration architect), Reena Racki, and Lee Carlson. In Pasadena, we thank Pasadena Heritage and Marguerite Duncan-Abrams, its program director, who introduced us to the Phelpses, two of its hardest-working and most loyal members. In addition, we appreciate the assistance and support of Jan Able, the leading preservation architect in Tampa, Florida.

Finally, to publisher Gibbs Smith and editor Theresa Desmond go our thanks for making an unusual commitment to the American Restoration Style series and the bungalow book in particular, which had some pretty uncompromising deadlines. To Forrest MacCormack, our photographic assistant and traveling companion, we thank you for hundreds of hours of talent and good company. And to one another, we say a boundless thank you, as always.

JAN CIGLIANO
WALTER SMALLING JR.
Washington, D. C.

Gustav Stickley oak sideboard in the Montgomery dining room, Hollywood, California. Stickley signed the pieces he designed, including this rustic buffet created during his experimental United Crafts period between 1901 and 1905 and unusual for its prominent butterfly peg motif in the cabinet doors and the strong geometry of the drawer pulls.

THE DESIGN HERITAGE

"THE BUNGALOW IS PLANNED AND BUILT TO MEET SIMPLE NEEDS IN THE SIMPLEST AND MOST DIRECT WAY." ■■ *Gustav Stickley, 1909* ■■ The bungalow epitomizes the adage that history repeats itself. America's love affair with the bungalow in the last decade echoes the enthusiasm that greeted the bungalow when it first arrived on the American scene in the early decades of the twentieth century. Our affinity with the heritage bungalow meshes with a renewed respect for the social and architectural values that mattered most when American families first embraced the bungalow in the 1910s and 1920s: living in a comfortable rather than a formal environment; using authentic materials in buildings and furnishings; designing objects and furnishings that respect functional form and simplicity in decor; and demanding natural, well-crafted artistry.

These values also coincide with other late-twentieth-century sentiments: a demand for excellent value for money spent; an enjoyment of our American heritage, whether in historic travel, historic period styles in houses and furnishings, old buildings and historic places, or antique furniture and fabrics; and a renewed pleasure in the outdoors and respect for environmental conservation. The bungalow, as an architectural model or house type, embodies these ideals of nature and craftsmanship. Indeed, it is a perfect fit for individuals who seek a sophisticated level of simplicity through artistic and crafted furnishings and home design.

The bungalow also offers a wonderfully attractive house genre for pleasant living: it is manageable in size, comfortably scaled, spacious and open in plan, relatively affordable to buy and maintain, and restful to the eye (with simple lines and natural tones and colors) as well as to the body (with easy movement within and through rooms). Walking into a vintage

bungalow of the 1910s or 1920s produces an immediate sense of ease because of the size, scale, and simplicity of the space. Yet living simply in the Arts and Crafts genre requires complex thought and adequate financial resources to plan, design, construct, and collect.

This book presents five exemplary bungalow houses around the country that represent different architectural styles, interior design influences, and lifestyle preferences. Each house, and the five together, provide a style guide of appropriate and economical design and a practical reference for maintaining, restoring, and furnishing an American bungalow, whether you live in a bungalow or seek to bring bungalow living into your home environment.

THE BUNGALOW DEFINED: A HOUSE TYPE

The term *bungalow* refers to a house type, just as a skyscraper or lighthouse refers to certain building types. Frequently associated with Gustav Stickley, the Arts and Crafts movement, and the Craftsman style, *bungalow* is often incorrectly used to describe a house in

the Craftsman, Mission, or Arts and Crafts style. Perhaps the greatest confusion arises when a four-square house in the Craftsman or Mission style is identified as a bungalow. Some of the confusion arises, no doubt, because both bungalow design and four-square house design encompass several of the same styles, including Craftsman, Mission, Spanish Colonial, Prairie, Colonial Revival and English Tudor.

Bungalow is a form of house, a type of structure designed in a number of architectural styles; *style* by contrast, is a particular period and genre of design. The bungalow house type is a single-family residence, one- or one-and-a-half stories high, and designed in elevation, plan, and roofline to achieve a horizontal and rectangular emphasis. The second floor, a modest space of one or two rooms or attic storage, is contained below the gable or hipped-roof area.

The American word *bungalow* comes from

The Alpha model bungalow, Sears, Roebuck & Co., Arlington, Virginia, built by a speculative developer and well maintained through the decades.

the British word *bangla,* actually referring to the East Indian people who lived in low, one-story thatched huts encircled by large porches. A term first used by British settlers in seventeenth-century India, the Hindi bangla offered a well-ventilated colonial dwelling with rooms opening off the airy central hall and verandahs on all sides. English colonialists who lived in bungalow dwellings in India gradually transformed the native version and transplanted the house type to the mother country. By the nineteenth century the bungalow had become quite popular around England's seaside resorts, and then widened its appeal during the seminal years of the English Arts and Crafts movement of the 1880s and 1890s. Bungalow design expressly emphasized fine craftsmanship and construction in natural materials. Eminent English Arts and Crafts designers, notably John Ruskin and William Morris, led the moral and humanist attack on materialism and consumer society to define tenets that became influential to American Arts and Crafts. They rejected machine-produced artifacts as gross and base, and demanded that building and furniture crafts be an expression of fine and decorative arts. Several European artists and designers in England, Austria, and Russia joined with Ruskin and Morris to promote their work as defined by the natural form of the object and material.

The appearance of the bungalow in America coincided with its emergence in England during the 1880s and 1890s, here along the eastern seaboard in resort and vacation towns as an inexpensive summer cottage. On the West Coast, small, one-story, Queen Anne-style cottages with breeze porches arose about the same time in neighborhoods around California and began to be favored by affluent winter residents traveling from the East and Midwest to southern California's temperate climate, notably in the resort town of Pasadena. The American Arts and Crafts movement gained a widespread following after the turn of the century, largely thanks to the impetus of Gustav Stickley (1858–1942), widely recognized as the major voice in the American Arts and Crafts movement and publisher of *The Craftsman* monthly magazine. And the bungalow house type came to exemplify Arts and Crafts virtues, albeit in a much different form than the original Anglo-Indian model developed in the English colony of India. Even while

THE IDEAL BUNGALOW DEFINED: AN AMERICAN HOUSE TYPE

■ ■ *Modest overall size and scale*

■ ■ *One or one-and-a-half story*

■ ■ *Second-floor area contained under roof structure*

■ ■ *Low to ground in appearance*

■ ■ *Rectangular or square shape*

■ ■ *Deep roof overhangs and wide eaves*

■ ■ *Porch across facade, or prominent in front, and on two or three sides*

■ ■ *Exterior typically composed of different materials*

■ ■ *Natural wood related to region or area*

■ ■ *Colors and tones related to nature and immediate environment*

■ ■ *Low gable roof with dormers*

This living room is characteristic of Craftsman- and Mission-style interiors, 1910–1930, particularly those affordably priced and built for middle-income families nationwide. The Arts and Crafts living room and central hearth are focused around the prominent brick fireplace (which the owner appropriately stripped of paint), framed by leaded-glass cabinets and artful windows above. Bungalow living rooms were furnished with chairs and small sofas to accommodate reading by, and talking among, individual family members, as opposed to many contemporary living rooms that are furnished with couches, easy chairs, and coffee tables for lounging and group entertaining.

some of Stickley's bungalow designs included plans that rose a full two stories, designed in the Craftsman style, most did indeed feature one- or one-and-a-half-story houses.

Stickley wrote in the 1909 *Craftsman* that the bungalow is "a house reduced to its simplest form, which never fails to harmonize with its surroundings, because its low broad proportions and absolute lack of ornament give it a character so natural and unaffected that it seems to sing into a blend with any landscape." And because it is built of local, natural materials, he concluded, "it is beautiful." Constructing a bungalow from regional materials remains an essential feature: wood-frame or cedar-shingle walls stained in a natural shade of brown or honey along the West Coast and in the southern states; stucco-daubed walls with tile roofs in the Southwest; brick walls and rolled asphalt roofing in the Midwest; or rounded

Arts and Crafts pottery often depicts motifs of nature and is displayed prominently on mantels, tables, and sideboards. This one in the Montgomery house was acquired from a local dealer.

IDEAL BUNGALOW VALUES

■ ■ *Simple*

■ ■ *Comfortable*

■ ■ *Nature's materials, colors, and forms*

■ ■ *Modest*

■ ■ *Crafted by artisans*

■ ■ *Integrated with the natural environment*

■ ■ *Affordable*

■ ■ *Art in form and function*

cobblestone in foundation walls and chimney stacks in the Mid-Atlantic region.

THE BUNGALOW'S DESIGNERS AND PATTERN BOOKS

Beyond Gustav Stickley's wide-ranging influence, voices in establishing bungalow stylistic design standards included Frank Lloyd Wright of Oak Park, Illinois, in the Midwest and the Chicago area, and Charles and Henry Greene of Pasadena, California, on the West Coast, all residential architects and designers of furniture, glass, tile, textiles, and metal objects that they integrated into the house's universal environment. Upstate New York, Chicago and the northern Midwest, and California came to be the influential enclaves for creative bungalow design. The brothers Greene & Greene had arrived in Pasadena at the dawn of the new century, seduced by the balmy climate, the imaginative frontier in living, and the affluent demand for residential architects. Even with their academic training in the classics, they created a signature style for bungalows and larger houses in southern California that flowed from the integrity of Japanese design, the nuances of the wooden architecture of Switzerland and southern Germany, and the historic roots of the California bungalow. For Greene & Greene and other California architects, the old Spanish adobe mission, simply built in harmony with the land, and all rooms opening to the outdoors and facing the U-shaped interior patio, provided the basic reference in this balmy climate.

During the same years that the works and bungalow designs of Stickley, Greene & Greene, and Frank Lloyd Wright flourished, the nation's middle class expanded exponentially. Ironically, industrialization fed this unprecedented economic growth. And there arose widespread desire to achieve the

American ideal of homeownership. Home-ownership increased by 4.7 million households between 1900 and 1920, a 100-percent increase in twenty years. The bungalow was the house of choice: affordable, appropriate for middle-income living, and in keeping with American's growing interest in nature.

The bungalow's affordability was matched by the ease of purchasing bungalow plans and building a bungalow, whether as a homeowner or a speculative builder. Bungalow building kits matched the mass availability of today's sewing patterns, widely available through popular magazines—*The Craftsman* (1901–1916), *Bungalow Magazine* (1909–1918), *Ladies' Home Journal*, and *House Beautiful*—and, most pervasive after 1909, such mail-order catalogs as Sears, Roebuck & Company, Montgomery Ward, and Aladdin Homes, which sold ready-cut homes and accounted for the greatest number of bungalows designed and built in America after 1910, followed by plan books and magazines.

Sears Roebuck offered more than twenty bungalow models in its catalog, *Book of Modern Homes and Building Plans* (1908), which was updated annually. It sent out plans, construction manuals, and materials to homeowners and contractors by rail. The notion of buying a home from a mail-order catalog was a new idea that captured the enthusiasm (and pocketbooks) of Americans quite rapidly in the early 1910s. Sears profited handsomely by offering one-stop shopping with attractive financing plans, producing more than 50,000 bungalows from 1908 to 1940, about half of all Sears houses in these years.

Americans loved the bungalow's spacious (and quite sociable) front porch, leaded-glass windows, oak staircases, and wooden detailing, as well as the flexibility to alter plans to suit the individual family's size and budget. Yet the purists, led by Stickley, felt the Sears and

The L. and J. G. Stickley oak armchair, paired in the living room above with a generic Mission-style rocker ordered from Montgomery Ward or Sears, Roebuck catalogs in the 1910s and 1920s, has in recent years commanded high prices among antique dealers.

Sears, Roebuck & Co. 1908 mail-order catalog.

Montgomery Ward prepackaged home kits diluted the regionalism in bungalow design by replacing local materials and bungalow designs adapted to their environment with precut lumber, nails, doors, and other "craftsman" parts sent by a central warehouse direct to the site. Yet across the country, middle-income homeowners and contractors on finite budgets made decisions based on economics rather than Stickley's aesthetic ideals, replacing higher-quality materials with less-expensive alternatives, and omitting craftsman woodwork, metalwork, and built-in furniture. Stickley's influence, even so, ran though every bungalow design in some way, whether it was only in one chair, a built-in bench or cabinet, or the fireplace. The designer's presence remains strong to this day, as evidenced by the popularity of furniture lines based on Stickley's name and principles.

Buying a Historic Bungalow

The Portners of Chicago, Illinois, one of the five homeowners featured in the book, are astute and experienced buyers of old houses and antique furnishings, and used their own inspection checklist when buying their Chicago bungalow. The excellence of this checklist—whether used by the purchaser or a professional inspection service for a modest fee—allows the buyer to avoid unexpected and usually expensive changes later:

■■ *Electrical wiring and circuits: Has the house been rewired in more than thirty years? If not, then budget for an extensive rework of the electrical wiring and sockets, and an upgrade of the electric power system.*

■■ *Plumbing systems and fixtures: Turn on faucets and flush toilets to check the cleanliness and pressure of water as well as the drainage. If the pressure is low, if toilets don't flush or take time and run, or if drains empty slowly, then the plumbing system will more than likely require repair. For older (and often lead) pipes, there will usually be a 10- to 20-percent increase in repair expenses.*

■■ *Floor strength and noise: To ensure structural stability and insulation between floors and rooms, walk the floor area of every room and jump in the center of the room. Any bounce in the floor suggests structural problems of weak beams or joists, and creaking may indicate rotten or thin floorboards.*

■■ *Wooden floors and trim: Dark spots may suggest water damage or rotting over time. Poke through paint or carpeting to determine the condition of wooden floors and trim, whether there is dry rot or termites, and whether the surfaces can be restored with refinishing and natural stain.*

■■ *Windows: Check the condition of all double-hung windows, casements, and French doors for the quality of the glass (wavy glass is preferable in early-twentieth-century bungalows), and whether they shut tightly and are easy to open and close. You should estimate the cost of repairs or ask a contractor to walk through.*

■■ *Heating and cooling: Are windows tight and secure to retain heat and cool air? Is the furnace gas or oil, or hot water steam? Is it fully operable or perhaps in need of replacement or expensive servicing? This is especially important to check when buying in warm weather. Is there air conditioning, a centralized system or window units? And what about insulation; is it sufficient? If not, ask the previous owner for average monthly heating and cooling costs, or estimate them yourself by calling the local utility.*

The Portner house, Chicago, Illinois, 1920, a characteristic Chicago bungalow. The front elevation of the bungalow, which typically has a horizontal thrust, instead is designed with a narrower width to accommodate the tighter Chicago city lot. The design achieves an angular emphasis through primary forms and materials: the band of four windows across the front, which correspond with four smaller leaded-glass windows; the golden brown brick construction; the angular shed-roofed dormer breaking the roofline; and the horizontal line of the side-facing gable roof, which the owners restored with dark brown asphalt to strengthen the bungalow's clean geometry and natural scale. The broad chimney stack reveals the prominence of the living-room fireplace, which extends along an entire end wall; the restored Prairie-style trellises in a geometric pattern highlight the historic integration of landscape and architecture.

BUNGALOW:
WHAT STYLE IS IT?

S TYLE IS A GOOD FRIEND WHEN PLANNING A REDESIGN OR RESTORATION OF YOUR HOUSE. WHETHER YOU ARE RE-CREATING THE ORIGINAL, ADAPTING the historic design to contemporary living, or adding a new use or more space, any and all alterations should respect the original scale and style. Style and scale guide decisions about exterior and interior design, materials, colors, and textures. Because bungalow styles across the country are strongly influenced by regional designers, climate, topography, the architectural vernacular, and such factors as

density and lot size, a windshield survey of similar houses in your area will provide essential references of local design patterns that could be incorporated in your restoration. If you have questions, consult a restoration designer or architect.

Most bungalows mix stylistic influences to great effect. In fact, one style may dominate the exterior, such as Colonial Revival or Swiss Chalet, while a complementary style influences the interior, such as Craftsman or Mission Revival. As restoration proceeds, numerous choices about stylistic direction and emphasis arise, options affecting the technical approach, architectural design, interior design, and fur-

nishings and accessories. Establishing this direction at the outset reduces the chances for budget overruns, and design and technical errors.

CRAFTSMAN STYLE (1900–1930)

In harmony with the environment, the Craftsman bungalow is designed, interior and exterior, for temperate climates, notably the southern states (North Carolina to Florida), California (especially the southern region), and the Southwest (where the sun shines two-thirds of the year). In Pasadena, home of the Phelps house, one of the five bungalows represented here, the Craftsman heritage bequeathed an enduring legacy in the nature of the materials and the integration with nature—the principal features that highlight the simple house form and minimal ornament. Broad, expansive porches, patios, and terraces, vine-covered pergolas, and groups of windows to bring in fresh air and a land of blue skies are common features in this popular bungalow style. The entire house and the low-pitched gable roof emphasize the horizontal line of the landscape. The building materials reflect this harmony: foundations, exterior walls, massive fireplaces, and chimneys are built of local stone; half-timbered wooden gables and exposed beams express the wooden construction; wall paneling and ceiling grids depict the nature of indigenous logs, cedar shakes, oak, and mahogany. Built-in furnishings include cabinets, sideboards, benches, and bookshelves.

The Chester house, Washington, D.C., is one of over 100,000 Sears, Roebuck & Co. kit houses built during 1908–1925, this one the popular "Elsmore" model, featuring deep bracketed eaves, windows all around, and a large front porch dominated by battered, or sloping, piers, in Arts and Crafts parlance known as "bungalow columns." Built by the first owners in 1919, the methodically restored Craftsman-style bungalow is featured throughout the book.

MISSION REVIVAL AND SPANISH COLONIAL REVIVAL (1890–1920)

The adobe architecture of eighteenth-century Spanish missions inspired Mission Revival design around the turn of the century in America, originating in the regions heavily settled by Hispanic natives, including Florida, California, New Mexico, and Arizona. Descended from the hacienda, buildings feature clean plain lines, virtually no ornament, and open patios in the center; more ornate designs dress up with rounded arches, high and curving gables, Moorish-style elements, and red-tiled roofs descended from vernacular church structures. Well-suited to the bunga-

low, Mission Revival design embodies the essence of simple living, natural materials, and the historic tradition of handcrafted workmanship. Moorish-style furniture and hardware, typically crafted in dark materials of mahogany and iron, are appropriate in the Mission Revival as well as other bungalow styles.

CALIFORNIA BUNGALOW (1905–1925)

The fusion of Craftsman and Spanish Mission influences found in old adobe haciendas and ranch houses produced the California bungalow, a popular West Coast style that capitalizes on the mild climate and the merging of the house with the land. Oriented to the outdoors and designed around a square or rectangular patio or courtyard, the California bungalow blends with the colors of its environment: golden dust, sandy desert, moss green, and rosy haze. Beauty emanates from the building's form and function, expressed in the natural appearance of structural elements and the high standards of craftsmanship. Ideally, the north-fac-

Mission Revival-style bungalow, O'Brien Court, San Jose, California, Historic American Buildings Survey rendering, 1990.

Mission Revival style, Tampa, Florida

The Phelps house in Pasadena, California, a classic California bungalow, built in 1908. Patron Lincoln Clark of Chicago, Illinois, came to Pasadena, a town that developed as a bungalow colony for eastern and midwestern migrants, for the temperate southern California climate. Los Angeles architect Frederick Roehrig designed this spacious and broad-slung bungalow, mixing Craftsman and Mission Revival elements in the West Coast bungalow genre that came to be known as California bungalow style.

ing entrance porch leads directly into the south-facing living room and opens out to the east-facing porch, the terrace, and the garden. The dining room flows from the living room through a large opening or doorway (of French doors or sliding pocket doors), and opens to a closed sunporch or walled, east-facing porch and patio. Most early California bungalows were originally built with the living-room fireplace as the only built-in heating source, intended as an economical design and a magnet for the family's communal living. Small fuel heaters warmed individual rooms.

PRAIRIE STYLE (1900–1920)

Frank Lloyd Wright introduced his Prairie-style house in 1901, noted for the horizontal spread across the flat midwestern landscape, or prairie, multiple and low-pitched roofs, broad eave overhangs, casement windows across facades, contrasting dark linear bands against lighter broad surfaces, short and squat chimney stacks, and minimal ornament so as not to detract from the overall composition's rectilinearity. Simultaneous with the rise of Wright and the Prairie School architects, the bungalow house type gained widespread favor among midwestern (and American) households. Prairie-style design complements bungalow design: open floor plans with prominent fireplaces, brick and brick-and-wood construction, and the Prairie style's banded trim on stucco. Beyond the midwestern states, Prairie-style bungalows appear in such distant regions as North Carolina and California. The Sears catalog promoted the Prairie-style bungalow as being "much favored by discriminating builders and found in the most exclusive communities."

CHICAGO BUNGALOW (1920–1930)

Tens of thousands of Chicago-area households built the so-called Chicago bungalow after 1900, mixing Prairie-style features with Craftsman and other Arts and Crafts influences. Created by Frank Lloyd Wright and Prairie School designers, the one-and-a-half-story Chicago bungalow is a simple house form, usually narrow across the front and longer in depth to fit dense subdivision lots within the city. Built of brick made in local factories, the Chicago bungalow can be identified by its splaying horizontal roofline, geometric art-glass motifs reminiscent of Wright's work, and internalized floor plans that appear protected from rather than open to the outdoors. Long and narrow floor plans arrange rooms back-to-back to minimize hallway space and concentrate living areas, therefore containing air drafts and economizing heating costs. Ornamental details are limited to leaded art-glass windows and unpainted wooden trim, such as that seen in this book in the Portner house of Chicago. Enclosed porches and sunrooms typically extend from the dining room or living room, at the rear or front of the house, their leaded-glass windows with geometric or floral motifs producing dramatic plays of colorful and natural light.

ENGLISH TUDOR REVIVAL STYLE (1890–1930)

The English Tudor Revival style, offering a good impression of Leicestershire, England, on a rainy day, is noted for steep pitched gables with half-timbering and stucco, an ivy-covered arch over the doorway, twin pent roofs, tall medieval chimneys, and diamond-shaped panes of glass in bay windows. Based on English farmhouses, thatched-roof cottages, and Tudor country manses, the English Tudor Revival style in America borrows stylistic details from the original structures, notably half-timbered detailing in gable ends, with dark timbers laid against white stucco or plaster surfaces. In the best Arts and Crafts vein, the English Tudor bungalow highlights the artistry of structural forms and building materials. Other telling traits are rounded roof eaves echoing thatched-roof forms, casement windows with small diamond panes, cobblestone (for chimneys, foundations, and porch columns), dark-stained timber or clapboard, and stuccoed daubing over frame or brick. English Tudor

Prairie style, Tampa, Florida

English Tudor Revival style

Revival bungalows in rustic and seaside areas can be found across the Mid-Atlantic states, Rhode Island to North Carolina.

COLONIAL REVIVAL (1910–1940)

The Colonial Revival (or neocolonial) bungalow became a favorite among tract homebuilders and pattern-book designers after 1900, an enthusiasm that coincided with Americans' renewed favor for classic and academic European designs. This bungalow offers

Colonial Revival style

This Swiss Chalet-style bungalow, designed by Los Angeles architect Arthur Kelly, emphasizes the natural woodenness of structural and artistic forms, featuring cutout wooden porch railings, exposed rafter ends, wide cedar porches and balconies, broad and low-slung roof gables touching tree boughs, and easy integration between nature and architecture, with the angular house plan guided by the steep and rocky site.

"an extremely dignified Colonial appearance, and [is] of substantial and warm construction," wrote Gustav Stickley in *The Craftsman*. Influenced by seventeenth-century New England colonial buildings, Colonial Revival-style bungalows, such as Sears' "Columbine"

and "Crescent" models, feature symmetrical massing, columnar porches, and classical details on the exterior, with the interior keeping with Arts and Crafts furnishings: dentiled roof gables, narrower overhangs, French doors, triple Palladian-like windows, six-over-six double-hung windows (rather than horizontal casements), and open porches with colonial-style railings. Interior plans and furnishings typically follow the Arts and Crafts tenets of open floors plans and built-in benches, sideboards, and cabinets.

SWISS CHALET (1900–1920)

The Swiss Chalet style distinguishes itself by its refined wooden detailing and wooden craftsmanship, especially that of the broad, dominant, front-facing gable. Decorative vergeboards, porch railings, exposed rafters, and vertical grooved boards recall the wooden houses of the Swiss Alps. California architects Charles and Henry Greene, who arrived in Pasadena in 1894, had actually studied the art of wooden architecture in Switzerland, and fellow architect Frederick Roerhig designed the first bungalow in Pasadena in the Swiss Chalet style in 1899. A manner well suited to interior-exterior integrated design, Swiss Chalet-style porches, balconies, sleeping porches, and wide overhangs provide sheltered open-air living spaces.

AIRPLANE BUNGALOW (1910–1930)

Shallow-sloping gables that look like airplane wings and extra-wide roof eaves suggest the spread of an airplane. The airplane bungalow is essentially styled in the Craftsman mode, typically one story with all rooms splaying across an expansive ground area. Designed to accentuate the lightness of crafted wood and the breezy openness of the generous window area and flowing plan, airplane bungalows tend to be found in areas where generous land lots remained low-priced during the early decades of the twentieth century, such as the southern states of the Carolinas, Georgia, and Florida.

THE FLOOR PLAN AND NATURAL DETAILS

The bungalow's *open floor plan* integrates the architectural structure with the interior design. In restoring a bungalow, furniture should harmonize with natural woodwork and built-in features. Refinishing *built-in furniture* will help to maximize space usage and enhance the sense of openness: window seats and glass-fronted cabinets in the living room, bookcases in the sitting room, a sideboard and china cabinets in the dining room, chests and closets in the bedroom and bathroom hallways.

It is the period-style bungalow that intro-duced the clever technique of using inner walls to conceal household utilities and service areas—such as stairways and closets, ironing boards and breadboards—to leave outer walls free for large windows. These houses, success-fully restored, are designed to be practical and efficient.

A common denominator in bungalow floor plans is the emphasis on openness, flexi-bility, and convenience of space usage. The bungalow's comfort derives from *unobstructed vistas* across and between rooms and the flow-ing circulation, with principal rooms opening into each other through wide, *wood-trimmed portals,* such as archways, double French doors, and simple thresholds.

WHAT STYLE IS IT?

CRAFTSMAN STYLE

- ■ ■ *Side-facing gable or cross-gabled roof*
- ■ ■ *Local stone foundation*
- ■ ■ *Low-pitched gable roof*
- ■ ■ *Wide eaves and exposed beams*
- ■ ■ *Crafted wooden details, exterior and interior*
- ■ ■ *Broad porches or patios, vine-covered pergolas*
- ■ ■ *Significant window area*
- ■ ■ *Wooden wall paneling and ceiling grids*
- ■ ■ *Fireplace inglenooks*
- ■ ■ *Built-in sideboards, benches, bookshelves*

CALIFORNIA BUNGALOW

- ■ ■ *Outdoor-indoor integrated*
- ■ ■ *Simplified Craftsman and Mission detailing*
- ■ ■ *Stucco or shingle exterior*
- ■ ■ *North-facing entrance porch*
- ■ ■ *South-facing living room and sun porch*
- ■ ■ *Central open-air courtyard or rear patio*
- ■ ■ *Significant window area*

CHICAGO BUNGALOW

- ■ ■ *Craftsman, Mission Revival, and Prairie style*
- ■ ■ *Brick construction*
- ■ ■ *One-and-a-half stories*
- ■ ■ *Narrower widths and longer depths for city lots*
- ■ ■ *Art-glass windows, floral or geometric motifs*
- ■ ■ *Crafted wooden trim and built-ins*
- ■ ■ *Narrower front porches*

SWISS CHALET

- ■ ■ *Woodenness emphasized, exterior and interior*
- ■ ■ *Large, front-facing gable*
- ■ ■ *Deep eaves*
- ■ ■ *Ornament derived from Swiss chalet houses*
- ■ ■ *Cutout moldings, verge-boards, beams*
- ■ ■ *Ornament in structural functions*
- ■ ■ *Cutout porch, balcony, sleeping porch railings*
- ■ ■ *Decorative and practical flower boxes*

ENGLISH TUDOR REVIVAL

- ■ ■ *English origins*
- ■ ■ *Rounded roof lines*
- ■ ■ *Half-timber details*
- ■ ■ *Trellises attached and next to house*

Restoration-style doorways and windows (external and within the house) typically favor an open, natural finish: *unpainted wood trim and curtainless windows.* In addition to honoring Arts and Crafts aesthetics, this enhances fresh-air circulation and natural light in these modestly scaled houses. Only bedrooms, bathrooms, and private studies or libraries are typically separated behind closed doors, as they are designed to be cozy and less open, cloaked with paint, paper, and curtains on walls, wood trim, and windows.

Restoration-style colors feature *deep and muted earth tones* to infuse the bungalow with a natural, subliminal calm: browns, greens, oranges, ochres, and reds. The rich hues of unpainted, naturally stained oak, pine, or mahogany in ceiling beams, wall paneling, built-ins, and French doors are intended to complement the pigments derived from the earth's resources of wood, flora and fauna, and sky and land, not the stark contrasts of whites and blacks. Complemented by textiles, textured wall coverings of brown or natural burlap, stenciling, or patterned paper, and lighted by the dim yellow glow of mica shades at night and the low rays of sun by day, the fusion of naturally stained woodwork against solid colors of crimson, moss green, terra-cotta, Pompeii red, and indigo blue produces comfortable and tranquil living environments.

COLONIAL REVIVAL

- *Neocolonial, Georgian, Federal-style details*
- *Symmetrical massing*
- *Classical porch columns and moldings*
- *Dentiled gable ends*
- *Triple (à la Palladian), double-hung, and diamond-paned windows*
- *Red brick with white trim or narrow clapboard siding*

MISSION REVIVAL AND SPANISH COLONIAL REVIVAL

- *Spanish, Portuguese, Indian influences*
- *Textured stucco walls*
- *Red-tile roof*
- *Influenced by 18th-century adobe Spanish missions*

- *Primitive detailing*
- *Front facade emphasized with arched, angled, or S-curved parapet or raised gable*
- *Roof dormers*
- *Deep roof overhangs*
- *Arcaded porches and patios*
- *Pergola entrances and patios*

PRAIRIE STYLE

- *Associated with Chicago bungalow and Frank Lloyd Wright*
- *Usually brick construction; stucco common*
- *Horizontal building lines*
- *Roofs appear flat; hipped roof with shallow pitch*
- *Deep eaves, often cantilevered*
- *Porches and terraces emphasize horizontal splay*

- *Super-sized square columns supporting porches*
- *Simple, geometric art-glass windows*
- *Large planters as architectural elements*

AIRPLANE BUNGALOW

- *One story*
- *Long, low-sweeping roofline like the jet's wingspread*
- *Raised attic level in large "dormer" element*
- *Very wide and shallow sloping gable roofs*
- *Deep roof overhangs and eaves*
- *Upswept gable peaks*
- *Wooden construction typical*

The Phelpses' covered entranceway suggests a larger porch by the exaggerated scale of the natural columns, the raised porte, the pergola-style hood, and the large, naturally stained door. Leading directly into the large living room, the west-facing doorway toward the side yard orients the living room and rear porch southward and the dining room and adjoining porch eastward. The Phelpses' tender restoration has encompassed the Craftsman ideal of enhancing the ornamental value of structural elements: cleaning and staining the charcoal-gray exposed rafter ends and deep green shingles, cleaning the small leaded-glass window, repainting the bright pumpkin window trim, and refinishing the wooden door and brass hardware.

FIVE BUNGALOWS:
RESTORATION STYLE MEETS PERSONAL STYLE

THE BUNGALOW'S FLEXIBLE AND LIGHT-FILLED FLOOR PLAN, COMFORTABLE SCALE, ARTISTRY, AND CRAFTSMANSHIP ARE HONORED IN CONTEMPORARY restoration designs that remain sympathetic to the spirit and scale of the original house. The five bungalows featured throughout the book offer living examples of the finest in practical maintenance and restoration. Their owners have succeeded in developing creative and affordable approaches to enhancing the beauty and the functionality of vintage houses for contemporary living. The houses

represent five popular bungalow styles including Craftsman, California, Chicago, Colonial Revival, and Swiss Chalet styles.

As a group, these houses highlight regional variations in building materials and architectural form, features which over time continue to influence restoration style decisions. We also see stylistic differences between the exterior and the interior, a common trait among American bungalows, such as a Craftsman-style exterior combined with a Colonial Revival-style interior, as in the Chester house. Throughout the country, one can find hundreds of examples of two-style bungalows, whether in Hendersonville, North Carolina; Santa Fe, New Mexico;

Salt Lake City, Utah; Tampa, Florida; Grand Rapids, Michigan; Seattle, Washington; or Des Moines, Iowa. Why this duplicity? Simply, the bungalow is a wonderfully flexible building form that adapts to many variables, style being one. Among the five bungalows, design styles include:

- ■ ■ Phelps house, Pasadena, California
  California-style exterior and interior
  Craftsman-style architectural details
- ■ ■ Chester house, Washington, D.C.
  Craftsman-style exterior
  Colonial Revival-style interior
- ■ ■ Portner house, Chicago, Illinois
  Chicago-style exterior and interior
  Eclectic Arts and Crafts-style details

The bungalow spirit emanates in the Phelps house of Pasadena, California. This 1910 photograph shows the original pergola and side fence bordering the entrance walk, shading visitors from the hot southern California sun.

■ ■ Browne house, Chicago, Illinois
   Colonial Revival-style exterior
   Craftsman-style interior
■ ■ Montgomery house, Hollywood,
      California
   Swiss Chalet-style exterior
   Mission Revival-style interior

The historic fabric and architectural style of these eighty- and ninety-year-old bungalows have been largely well cared for by different owners who have upgraded, altered, painted, and changed the use of rooms and spaces. (Exceptions are noted throughout for each house.)

Restoration work by the present owners is featured room by room in each chapter of the book. Each owner has made restoration and interior-design decisions after research into the house's history and careful study of the architecture and of appropriate restoration techniques and approaches. They respect Arts and Crafts fundamentals, the craftsmanship of wood, metal, masonry, pottery, fabrics, and paints and papers, appreciating as they do stylistic motifs and nuances of the art and architecture. While they are knowledgeable collectors and respectful adherents to the bungalow's tenets, they also live contemporary lives that require certain adaptations in houses built almost a century ago.

Except for the Montgomery house, financial constraints have guided the owners in their decisions about individual restoration projects, each making informed personal choices about the scope of work to be completed at certain times and also about the parts of the house requiring a greater or lesser investment of resources, such as exterior walls, roof surfaces, dormers, living room, dining room, bathroom, wiring, and windows.

The owners' restoration choices typically reflect:

■ ■ the structural condition of the bungalow when they acquired it;

■ ■ changes in the house's condition that have emerged over time; and,

■ ■ personal observations about particular features that have greater or lesser significance to the house's architectural presentation and to the family's way of life.

Structural failure usually dictates priority attention in restoration or rehabilitation projects, such as a leaking roof, a rotting foundation, frayed electrical wiring, structural settlement, or attic air circulation. Design and decorative upgrades usually result in greater aesthetic impact, but they take lower priority over the stabilization of the historic structure.

THE BUNGALOWS AND THEIR HOMEOWNERS

■ ■

PHELPS HOUSE, PASADENA, CALIFORNIA
CALIFORNIA BUNGALOW-STYLE
EXTERIOR AND INTERIOR

The House's History

Built in 1908 for Lincoln Clark, an easterner from Massachusetts by way of Chicago, the Phelps house was designed by architect Frederick Roehrig, who designed Pasadena's first Craftsman-style house in 1899. Pasadena had become a spa town for easterners, and in time, such affluent winter residents as the

RESTORING THE BEAUTY OF AGE'S PATINA

"I want to maintain the patina of the 'aged' house," movie producer Monty Montgomery, known for Portrait of a Lady (1997) and Blue Velvet (1986), told his restoration architect Martin Eli Weil and contractor Tim Kelly. *"I want a place that is non-L.A."*

Montgomery had managed the restoration of his former Adirondack-style fishing lodge in upstate Connecticut, and he wanted some of that rustic feel to be restored in this Swiss Chalet- and Mission-style bungalow. He looked for an architect who shared his sensitivity to restoration and authentic circa-1910 construction. He found it in Los Angeles architect Martin Eli Weil, known for impeccable period restorations.

The restoration designer and contractors restored the beautiful tawny patina of the aged bungalow with a close-knit team of craftspeople and artisans, including landscape architect Sara Munster; Arts and Crafts designer Roger L. Conant Williams; lighting designer Michael Adams; craftsman Atli Ararson; hardware artisan Bud Wolski; rug dealers Joley Kelter and Michael Malce; and the memories and photographs of Kate Frost Tufts, daughter of the original owner.

The heart of the team was Weil's restoration design and contractor Tim Kelly's craftsmanship. It is the six core employees that work full-time for Kelly that are the key to his fine technical restorations, people committed to quality and reputation, encompassing the skills of carpentry, framing, painting, moldings, graining and finishes, and management.

Lincoln Clarks, the Rand McNallys, and the David Gambles set off a building surge as they moved permanently to this sunny climate. The Craftsman, Mission, and California bungalow styles led the architectural fashion, their popularity solidified by the patronage houses of architects Roehrig and Charles and Henry Greene, and builders Arthur and Alfred Heinemann.

Roehrig, a native of New York state and son of German-born academics, trained in classical architecture at Cornell University. He opened his architectural practice in Pasadena in 1886, and then moved it to Los Angeles in 1890, establishing his reputation as a prodigious designer of many architectural styles.

Architectural Features

The impeccable features of this California bungalow include the following:

■■ broad low-pitched gable roof facing north;

■■ wide eaves supported by exposed beams;

■■ shingled exterior walls, stained deep forest green;

■■ ground-floor plan emphasizing cross-circulation and open-air ventilation;

■■ one-story original plan featuring five rooms on ground level, including living room, dining room, kitchen with pantry, two bedrooms, and one bathroom; full-floor attic area under broad roof structure built-out as second-floor bedrooms in 1941;

■■ integrated outdoor and indoor spaces, notably original vine-covered pergola along entrance walk and second-story window boxes, and broad porches and patios opening out from living room and dining room;

■■ large window area on all facades and sun-filled interior spaces;

BEFORE YOU RESTORE: RESEARCH YOUR HOUSE'S HISTORY

■■ *Search for physical additions and alterations visible to the eye—a flashlight is key.*

■■ *Floor plans may have been altered, walls moved or changed, ceilings or floors lowered, raised, or removed.*

■■ *The architect's original drawings or the builder blueprints may be available.*

■■ *Deed records, found in the local Office of the Recorder, are public record and enable the tracing of the house's property owners over time; they might also indicate the year the house was built.*

■■ *Tax Assessment records indicate, by a jump in property value, when the house was built.*

■■ *Building permit records, located at the local Building Permit or Zoning office, might have the original house plans.*

■■ *City directories, indexed by address, identify who occupied the house; early-twentieth-century directories can be found at the local historical society or public library.*

■■ *Historic photographs and lithographs show the original features and changes to the house.*

■■ *Sanborn Insurance maps for individual jurisdictions outline the houses on each street; the Library of Congress, Washington, D.C., is a central repository.*

■■ *Family papers and personal records of former owners might identify physical changes to the house or how earlier owners used certain rooms.*

■■ *Obituaries and newspaper articles might profile the former owners or feature the house or street.*

The Phelps house before restoration, living room open to rear porch, and dining room.

■■ naturally stained oak trim in living room, never painted;

■■ fireplace inglenook integrated into living-room area and framed by built-in bench;

■■ natural oak wall paneling and ceiling beams in dining room, never painted; and,

■■ built-in sideboard with glass-front cabinets and leaded casement windows above in east-facing dining room.

Restoration Style

When Lew and Cathy Phelps, the fourth owners, bought this Craftsman-style California bungalow in 1986, they walked into what looked like a "1970s modernization," says Cathy. The previous owner had remodeled the interior by removing the original dining-room plate rail and replacing the hardwood oak floors in the living room and dining room with contemporary tongue-in-groove, wide-board floors. They had furnished with Victorian reproductions and had opened the living room and rear porch into one space, installing a hot tub in the porch area.

The Phelpses decided the broad gable roof needed to be replaced and the shingle-shake siding required cleaning, resealing, and staining. Over twelve years, they have methodically restored in phases. They completed major structural improvements first, then restored, step by step, principal architectural features affecting the exterior stylistic character, such as the shingle siding, continuing with interior rooms as finances permit. The Phelps' restoration has encompassed:

■■ replacing rotted shingles and restaining shingled exterior surfaces;

■■ replacing shingled asphalt roof, and reversing color scheme of roof and shingle walls: original forest green roof reshingled with dark brown asphalt, and dark brown shingle wall restained deep forest green;

■■ repainting window and doorway trim with a brighter pumpkin orange than the original muted burnt orange, a livelier, contemporary look that respects period color schemes;

■■ furnishing principal ground-floor rooms (living and dining room, fireplace inglenook, and guest room) with Craftsman furnishings, wallcoverings, paint, and finishes;

■■ restoring living-room wall and floor surfaces, including oak wall paneling and golden ochre grass-cloth wall covering;

■■ restoring dining-room walls to match ochre grass-cloth covering in the living room, an appropriate finish yet lighter than original olive-yellow burlap when artificially lit;

▪▪ restoring original Craftsman-style French doors between living room and south-facing rear porch, and dining room and east-facing porch, to establish indoor-outdoor separation and create light-filled connections; previous owner had removed and stored doors to unify space in living room and porch and to install hot tub in porch area;

▪▪ recreating dining-room plate rail, which previous owner removed; restoration architect William Ellinger helped Lew Phelps design rail by interpreting historic photographs;

▪▪ renovating first-floor guest room in Craftsman style with Bradbury & Bradbury papers on walls and ceiling and furnishing with early-twentieth-century family pieces;

▪▪ relandscaping large backyard with period-style garden and poolside benches and chairs.

Projects yet to be completed include:

▪▪ renovating kitchen and restoring original cabinets;

▪▪ restoring south-facing enclosed porch off living room and open-walled, east-facing porch leading out from dining room;

▪▪ restoring original ground-floor bathroom;

▪▪ rebuilding pergola along entrance walk;

▪▪ relandscaping front yard and garden in period style.

CHESTER HOUSE, WASHINGTON, D.C.
CRAFTSMAN-STYLE EXTERIOR AND COLONIAL REVIVAL-STYLE INTERIOR

The House's History

Built in 1917–1918 from a Sears, Roebuck & Co. "Elsmore" model house kit, the Chester house is one of hundreds of bungalows in the Washington, D.C., area dating from the early twentieth century. It remains among precious few, however, that retain much of the original character, a near-idyllic Sears bungalow.

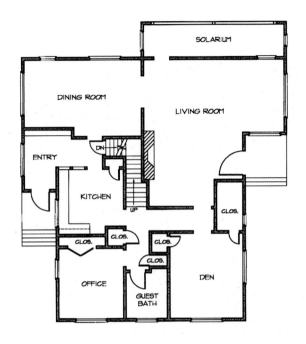

The Phelps house floor plan. The living room forms the heart of the floor plan, opening into the dining room and separated by a short rear hallway from the two principal bedrooms at the front of the house, the bathroom, and the kitchen. The house is designed to maximize fresh-air circulation with cross-ventilation between rooms, from the rear porch, across the living room, and through the operable leaded-glass windows framing the fireplace inglenook and rear hallway. The simplicity of the Phelpses' restoration calls for windows without curtains, which enhances the Craftsman style, as well as fresh-air ventilation.

This architectural rendering of the front elevation of the Chester house highlights battered, or sloping, columns in bungalow design, a popular feature nationwide. This hearth-oriented bungalow centers around the wide front porch and the large front living room. The owners carefully selected a contrasting color scheme of muted tones—cream, ivory, and forest green—to heighten the effect of shapes, textures, and forms; the stuccoed gable ends and porch columns; the ornamental timber framing; and the deep bracketed eaves.

This detail of the Chester house roof eave and exposed bracket highlights the impact of this single architectural element on the overall design and scale of the bungalow.

The first owners ordered the Elsmore kit with most of the upgrade options available in the catalog, including hardwood floors and trim, walnut woodwork in the living room and dining room, top-grade thick plaster walls, and a classic doorway and window trim in the broken-pediment pattern, a special Sears feature during 1916–1921. This modest-sized bungalow stood superior in design and quality to neighboring Sears houses on the street, which speculative builders had constructed for the least cost for resale, opting for the base model with no upgrades.

In 1988, the Chesters acquired the Sears bungalow and set about restoring it to the vintage home it was built to be. With discriminating eyes for design and the historic house's fine details, they adapted the flexible floor plan to the informal living style of two working professionals who relax by cooking together and entertaining friends, family, and frequent out-of-town guests.

RESTORATION CHALLENGES IN A BUNGALOW*

CONTEMPORARY LIVING CHALLENGES:

■ ■ *Living with low light levels, especially after sundown (pp. 49, 52-57, 100)*

■ ■ *Installing a second bathroom in a historic one-bathroom interior (pp. 81, 83-84)*

■ ■ *Ventilating and insulating the attic half-story (p. 79)*

■ ■ *Building more storage space (pp. 73, 85, 89)*

■ ■ *Building out the second-floor half-story into living space (pp. 79, 83, 96)*

■ ■ *Designing restoration-style house additions (pp. 70-72)*

■ ■ *Kitchen renovation: modern versus period-style appliances (pp. 65-69, 74-75, 102)*

DECORATING QUESTIONS:

■ ■ *Appropriate window treatments (pp. 47-49)*

■ ■ *Carpeting: Orientals? Wall-to-wall? Native American? (pp. 50-57, 67, 75, 76, 94)*

■ ■ *Creating a coffee table in the authentic Craftsman style (p. 51)*

■ ■ *Authentic Arts and Crafts pieces vs. reproductions (pp. 56, 73)*

■ ■ *Restoration-style colors (pp. 53-54, 57, 62, 73, 86, 91, 97-98, 108-109)*

■ ■ *Restoration-style fabrics (pp. 57, 91, 103, 108-109)*

■ ■ *Restoration-style wallpapers and stenciling (pp. 36, 55, 67, 71, 84, 92, 107, 108-109)*

* *and practical solutions on these pages*

Architectural Features

Sears promoted the Elsmore model as a "graceful bungalow, well lighted and ventilated." Features include the following:

■ ■ one-and-a-half stories with a combination gable and hip roof;

■ ■ broad front-facing gable with wide bracketed eaves and spacious front porch;

■ ■ exterior walls of clapboard, pebble-stucco front-porch columns and broad gable ends (front, side, and rear), and timber-frame deco-

USING OLD ELEMENTS IN NEW ADDITIONS

"We reused as many of the old parts as we could salvage during the renovations," says Ms. Chester, "all the original pine flooring in the kitchen, the old enamel sink from the back powder room, and all the original radiators." True to the spirit of this eighty-year-old bungalow, each restoration project and the additions to the kitchen and the second-floor bedroom area integrate original architectural elements, old parts salvaged from another part of the house and relocated to newly built or restored areas.

An original enamel bathroom sink was reinstalled in the new period-style bathroom off the kitchen; an original radiator was moved from a former room to a newly renovated room; and wood trim in the original house has been recreated in renovated rooms as well as in the new kitchen addition.

The result of reusing and re-creating original architectural design elements is a seamless tie between the old and new spaces of the historic bungalow in spirit, scale, and style.

rative pattern overlaid on gable ends;

■ ■ open floor plan: no hallways, and rooms flowing into one another;

■ ■ interior doorways and windows framed by dark-stained walnut trim in broken pediment design;

■ ■ one-story original plan with five principal rooms on ground level, including two bedrooms, one bathroom, living room, dining room, kitchen, and small rear utility porch;

■ ■ central living room with walnut ceiling beams and prominent end fireplace, originally framed by built-in bookcases and small square windows above, removed circa 1930;

■ ■ freestanding, one-car "utility" garage, a Sears mail-order model.

Restoration Style

Over ten years, the Chesters have completed one carefully planned restoration in 1993, five years after purchasing, and one emergency restoration in 1997, after a tree fell

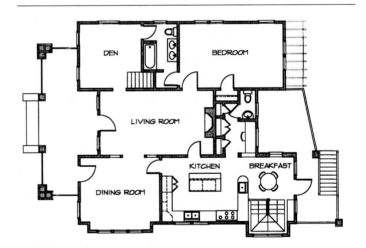

The Chester house floor plan epitomizes efficiency and openness with no hallways, and rooms flowing one into the other throughout the ground floor. Still, privacy in the master bedroom, rear, is assured, as it is in the family's kitchen area and breakfast nook to the rear. The one original bathroom, adjoining the two bedrooms, has been renovated for contemporary use and supplemented by a half bath at the rear and full bathrooms in the built-out upstairs area under the roof and in the basement guest room.

Nature provided the impetus for the Chesters' second renovation.

decade. Overall the Chesters have completed the following areas:

■ ■ kitchen renovation and addition of 120-square-foot breakfast nook and rear stair, including adding work stations for two cooks and large central island; rebuilding and replacing original Sears built-in cabinetry; and repairing water-damaged Georgia heart-pine floor with newly milled pine from North Carolina;

■ ■ kitchen "pantry" expansion, including renovating the original rear utility porch (which had been insulated with 1930s newspapers) into a new half-bathroom, a desk area for daily household paperwork, and a bank of Sears-styled storage cabinets;

■ ■ restoration-style half bathroom, featuring 1930s enamel sink, original radiator, and a reproduction mirror adapted from the house's historic Sears wood trim;

■ ■ basement guest room with bathroom, accessible from kitchen stairway and rear terrace through period-style double French doors;

■ ■ period-style rear deck and pergola, in keeping with scale of original front porch, and new rear gable to match front gable, bracketed eaves, and timber-frame ornament;

■ ■ second-floor trunk room restored as low-ceilinged guest room under large front gable;

■ ■ restored and replaced roof after tree damage, raised side hip-roof slope to a modified gable, expanding useable space under second-floor roof eaves and building-out rear shed dormer;

■ ■ restored and expanded first-floor master bedroom by opening it into original sleeping porch; added vintage-style Sears cabinets and window and door trim;

■ ■ renovated master bathroom (between ground-floor bedrooms) in period style, with beaded paneled wainscoting, porcelain tile floor, Sears-style wood trim, and original radiator.

through the roof and master-bedroom wall during a torrential rainstorm on April 1. For both projects, they worked closely with Blackburn Architects of Washington, D.C., project architect James Pandula, to correct unsympathetic earlier additions and alterations. Overall they restored and added new spaces in keeping with the scale and detail of the original house while integrating the requirements of an informal domestic life.

In the first restoration, the Chesters integrated the house with its site by shifting the household's main living area from the front of the house—the central porch and hearth-oriented living room—to the rear—the renovated kitchen and the enlarged breakfast room, a basement guest room, and an expanded outside deck, pergola, and rear terrace.

The second restoration repaired and raised the roof to build-out the second-floor guest bedroom with a full bathroom adjacent, and restored the master bedroom and bathroom on the ground level. They have also completed smaller restoration projects throughout the

PORTNER HOUSE, CHICAGO, ILLINOIS
CHICAGO BUNGALOW-STYLE
EXTERIOR AND INTERIOR

The House's History

Built in 1920 by Chicago architect Theodore Steuben and builder A. Petzald, the Portners' one-and-a-half-story brick bungalow stands in Chicago's northwestern subdivision known as the Villa, a six-block area of boulevards developed between 1907 and 1922. This National Register for Historic Places district showcases an array of bungalow styles. Five families have owned and occupied the Portner house across eight decades.

Architectural Features

This Chicago Bungalow style, designed to accommodate the narrow Chicago city lot, mixes Craftsman- and Prairie-style features on the exterior with a classic Arts and Crafts interior. Elements include the following:

■■ one-and-a-half-story, golden brown brick structure with sienna red tile roof;

■■ large Chicago-style picture window on front facade, with groups of casement and double-hung windows, and colorful leaded-glass windows all around;

■■ small front-entrance porch leading into enclosed vestibule and separate foyer, designed to contain cold Chicago air and prevent drafts from flowing into adjoining living room;

■■ woodenness emphasized in natural oak living room, mahogany dining room, and birch sunroom;

■■ efficient floor plan with minimal hall area and open room flow;

■■ large living room dominated by Craftsman-style brick fireplace, flanked by glass-fronted built-in cabinets and colorful art-glass windows above;

■■ built-in window seats along living-room and dining-room picture windows, concealing steam radiators;

The Portner house, located in a National Register for Historic Places district in Chicago.

The Portner house entrance vestibule displays colorful leaded-glass windows, an artistic space that has the practical purpose of shielding the adjacent living room from cold-air drafts for six months of the year, as well as providing a place to hang coats and store boots and umbrellas.

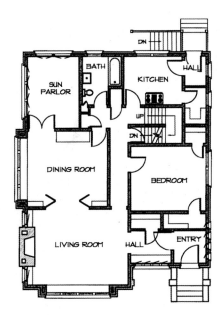

The Portner house floor plan demonstrates an efficient use of space, with rooms flowing into one another while separate functions and privacy are assured. Indicative of the higher quality of the design and the value of this house, the large dining room leads into a rear sunroom, which might be used for informal family dining and quiet reading, as well as to a small private library to the side.

■■ sunroom opening directly off dark mahogany dining room;

■■ original first-floor enamel-and-tile bathroom.

Restoration Style

When the Portners bought this Chicago bungalow in 1990, they walked into a pristinely maintained house filled with colorful, leaded art-glass windows and naturally stained oak, birch, and mahogany rooms with oak floors and built-in furniture. It is an excellent remnant of the architect's and contractor's artful design and the subsequent owners' diligent care. Fortunately, the crafted wooden surfaces had never been painted, and previous owners had even retrieved the two original trellises, part of the architect's original design, and restored them to the front yard. Unsympathetic alterations are relatively modest, including the upstairs master bathroom, a contemporary space that rises to break the roofline

through a shed dormer (unnoticeable from the front), a cedar deck attached to the rear, and a "modernized" 1980s kitchen.

The Portners, avid collectors of authentic Arts and Crafts pieces, have completed the following restoration projects:

■■ painting rooms in muted tones to complement dark wood trim;

■■ incremental and thorough rewiring of all sockets, fixtures, and outlets, completed by a professional electrician;

■■ repairing and retiling roof with sienna red tiles to define the low-pitched gable and complement the golden brown brick exterior;

■■ furnishing rooms in an eclectic mix of early-twentieth-century American and English Arts and Crafts furniture, fixtures, and accessories, and complementary Mission Revival, Moorish, Deco, and Nouveau pieces;

■■ collecting fine Arts and Crafts furniture and accessories as well as Roseville Pottery from local dealers, newspapers ads, and out-of-town antique markets on an ongoing basis.

Projects yet to be completed include the following:

■■ replacing rear deck with a sympathetic, rectangular, walled bungalow porch;

■■ landscaping the side driveway and rear yard as a garden, following early-twentieth-century landscape and plant charts.

BROWNE HOUSE, CHICAGO, ILLINOIS
COLONIAL REVIVAL-STYLE EXTERIOR AND CRAFTSMAN-STYLE INTERIOR

The House's History

The Browne house, built in 1916 by a local homebuilder, might easily be mistaken for a traditional turn-of-the-century residence, due to its plain, white-stuccoed, Colonial Revival-style exterior trimmed by dark forest green on windows and roof cornices. The house's narrower, more vertical thrust (a characteristic feature of the Chicago Bungalow style) and the steeper-pitched double-gable roof also seem to promise a neocolonial interior. Yet the interior is anything but traditional. It is solidly Craftsman style.

Gus and Jane Browne acquired the bungalow in 1974. Previous owners had maintained the house quite well across eight decades, though they had completely painted over the beautiful nutty-brown oak hardwood trim around the windows and doors. The Brownes reversed this desecration and restored the natural Craftsman woodenness of rooms and surfaces with systematic care.

Architectural Features

Located in one of Chicago's close-in residential suburbs, this bungalow features the following:

■ ■ one-and-a-half-story plan with minimal hallway space;

■ ■ Colonial Revival-style exterior and Craftsman-style interior;

■ ■ an exterior of brick construction daubed with stucco, painted a flat white and dark green rather than deeper, contrasting Arts and Crafts tones;

■ ■ a large and sun-filled oak hardwood living room centered around the fireplace and integrated with the front sunporch (originally separated by French doors);

■ ■ oak-paneled dining room integrated with the living room through a wide opening;

■ ■ original first-floor tile-and-enamel bathroom;

■ ■ exquisite Stickley, Craftsman, and Mission Revival furnishings and accessories, antique and reproductions, throughout.

Restoration Style

For twenty-four years, the Brownes have invested the majority of available time and money in restoring the warm patina of interior

The "front" doorway of the Browne house. Facing out to the side driveway, the entrance leads into an open, natural oak entrance hall, then up to the living room. The raised, three-stair entrance foyer effectively elevates the main level, an unusual treatment in the bungalow plan, perhaps created to raise the ground floor off the cold Chicago ground. The owner's restoration design infuses a domestic warmth into the existing ceremonial space by filling wall spaces with personal treasures: portraits of Civil War generals above and over the door; a large turn-of-the-century mirror framed by fluted columns; a hanging hat rack; a Craftsman-style side chair and lamp re-created by designer Louis Bussman; and inexpensive wool throw rugs adapted by Carson Pirie Scott from a familiar Arts and Crafts rose pattern, circa 1910.

spaces and architectural features. The exterior, by contrast, remains aesthetically uninspiring with a severe, white-stuccoed surface that minimizes light-and-shadow contrasts of exterior forms. Yet it is structurally sound. Over time, the Brownes have methodically completed numerous projects, all thoughtfully planned and most executed by the Brownes, in tandem with their longtime carpenter and craftsman, Tony Aducci of Berwyn, Illinois:

■ ■ stripping white enamel paint off windows, moldings, paneling, fireplace mantel, and other wooden surfaces, board by board, win-

The Browne house, Chicago, Illinois, built in 1916 by a local contractor, similar to thousands of bungalows in the Chicago area during the 1910–1930 period. The plainly styled Colonial Revival exterior, brick daubed with stucco and painted in a low-relief ivory white that longs for a deeper palette of colors for higher contrasts, exhibits the vertical emphasis of the Chicago Bungalow style. The drama and comfort of Arts and Crafts styling are fully revealed in the beautifully restored Craftsman-style interior. Previous owners had integrated the enclosed front porch, facing south and projecting out from the main block, into the spacious living-room area, flooding the bungalow's principal room with natural light.

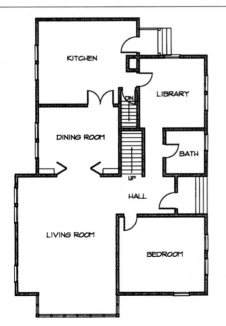

The Browne house floor plan depicts a hearth-centered environment, the fireplace on axis with the front door and the living room/dining room open to all functions, served by the kitchen and supported by two bedrooms and a bathroom.

dow by window, year by year;

■ ■ restoring Craftsman-style furnishings and wall coverings to all interior rooms and common spaces with professional-level care and quality, assisted by carpenter Aducci and Arts and Crafts designer Paul Duchscherer, San Francisco;

■ ■ building-out second-floor attic space with television sitting room and master bathroom designed in contemporary Mission-inspired style, adjoining master bedroom;

■ ■ collecting authentic and reproduction Mission- and Craftsman-style furniture, textiles, artwork, china, and pottery on an ongoing basis.

MONTGOMERY HOUSE,
HOLLYWOOD, CALIFORNIA
SWISS CHALET-STYLE EXTERIOR AND
MISSION REVIVAL-STYLE INTERIOR

The House's History

Dr. C. L. Frost retained Los Angeles architect Arthur R. Kelly in 1905 to design this spacious, Swiss Chalet-style bungalow high in Hollywood's desert hills. Construction was completed in 1911. Dr. Frost lived in the bungalow for fifty-five years until he died in 1966. His daughter Kate Frost Tufts then acquired the house with her husband. In the 1980s, Mrs. Tufts decided to donate her lifetime home to Claremont College rather than invest in an extensive restoration of the foundation, exterior walls and roof, interior spaces and surfaces, and the site. Claremont, as well, had minimal funds to restore the house and maintained its status-quo condition. Then film producer Monty Montgomery discovered the gem in 1993.

Claremont had not placed the bungalow on the market, but Montgomery, searching for a residence that offered comfortable ambiance rather than L.A. panache, discovered the run-down Frost house and negotiated with Claremont to buy and restore it. Rustic yet elegant, the superb architectural design fit perfectly with Montgomery's tastes and his interest in a house to "redo," having previously restored an Adirondack-style fishing lodge and camp in upstate Connecticut. He soon befriended Mrs. Tufts, who shared her memories of the house along with boxfuls of photographs.

Architectural Features

Built into the steep granite terrain and surrounded by big succulent cacti, the Montgomery house, renamed Mariposa, stands as an integrated design of architecture and landscape, splaying horizontally across the hillside, the ground floor fanning out at soft and wide angles, not boxed into a clean rectangle of sharp angles. The floor plan reflects the irregular site: extending to one side off the entrance hallway are the living room and dining room (stepping down), kitchen and pantry, and maid's room (stepping up), and a small library and study to the other. Under the low-sloping gable roof, the upper floor houses the master bedroom, two small bedrooms, and two bathrooms.

Architectural features to note:

■■ rises one-and-a-half stories to follow the slope of the hill, visibly lifted above the high stone foundation;

■■ Swiss Chalet-style exterior, Mission Revival-style interior;

■■ follows the Feng Shui philosophy of house design, in which the orientation of the master bedroom, kitchen, and living room (east, east and south, and south) are perfectly sited for serenity and healthful living;

■■ woodenness emphasized, from the original dark-stained cedar-shake shingles on exterior walls to the natural oak and fir interior surfaces and trim;

■■ large front-facing gable;

■■ wide roof overhangs, extending the building lines and creating shade at midday in the hot sunny climate;

The Montgomery house, sited in the steep foothills of Hollywood, California, built circa 1910, and designed in the Swiss Chalet style on the exterior and Mission Revival style on the interior by architect Arthur Kelly, an early apprentice of Greene & Greene. The impeccable restoration, 1993–1995, features wide, protective eaves, bracketed gables, and cutout porch railings intertwined with the vegetation of the landscape in this cedar-shingled structure. Magnificent window areas open into rustic yet elegant Mission Revival spaces, emphasizing the natural woodenness of honey-toned oak surfaces and the architect's perfect execution of the Feng Shui philosophy of home design: corners smooth and rounded, not sharp or abrupt, and the living room facing south, the dining room and kitchen east, and the master bedroom east and south and integrated with nature through the screened-in sleeping porch. Movie producer Monty Montgomery bought the house in 1993 and named it Mariposa, after a poem by patron Dr. C. L. Frost's son-in-law.

■■ decorative cutout gable vergeboards, porch and balcony railings;

■■ structural elements as part of the ornamental design, such as exposed roof rafters;

■■ porches, terraces, and stone patios (or arbors) leading out from the house on all sides to create multiple indoor-outdoor connections and outdoor living spaces;

■■ an enclosed screened-in porch opening off the dining room from inside and the front open porch from outside;

■■ a sleeping porch off the second-floor master bedroom, now a day office.

The Montgomery house living room before restoration.

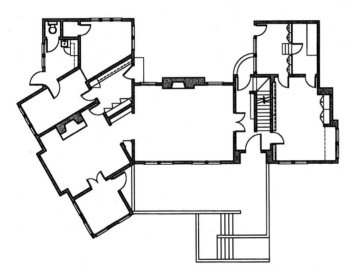

The Montgomery floor plan reflects the integration of house and landscape, fanning out across the hillside at soft and wide angles.

Restoration Style

With a love for large and creative projects, movie producer Monty Montgomery decided to restore the house and grounds in one major effort. Having studied the early Frost photographs and Arthur Kelly's original architectural drawings, he retained Los Angeles restoration architect Martin Eli Weil and contractor Tim Kelly, both coming off a "pure" museum-quality renovation for David O. Selznick. Montgomery suggested that museum quality was inappropriate for this eighty-year-old cedar-and-oak bungalow. Instead, he asked Weil and Kelly to restore the patina of the aged house.

The design team also included Roger L. Conant Williams, curator and Arts and Crafts consultant to Weil and Montgomery, and landscape architect Sarah Munster, who thoroughly stripped and partially replanted the ten-acre site. The success of Tim Kelly's building and restoration work centers on his diligence and his core team of six salaried employees who work with him on every job, including a carpenter, base electrician, wood finisher/grainer, and superintendent who oversees framing, painting, and moldings. Kelly also adhered to the crafts and techniques that would have been used during construction in 1905–1911, tracking down period materials, woods, and glass as well, an exceptional restoration standard that Montgomery insisted on. The carpenter repaired the foundation and framing systems with 4-by-6 hand-sawn pine rather than machine-sawn 2-by-4 boards. One-and-a-half years of rebuilding and restoration encompassed the following:

- ▪▪ rebuilding foundations;
- ▪▪ replacing, cleaning, and restaining exterior cedar-shake walls;
- ▪▪ removing the original shake roof, sealing the surface, and replacing it with rolled tar-paper roofing, a favorite roof covering of Greene & Greene in the early twentieth century, to comply with Los Angeles County fire codes that prohibit wood for roof material;
- ▪▪ comprehensive refinishing and restoration of interior rooms and spaces;
- ▪▪ rebuilding original bookcases that Dr. Frost's daughter had removed;
- ▪▪ refinishing the honey-toned oak floors and ceiling beams;
- ▪▪ installing Mission- and Craftsman-style

STEPS TO SUCCESSFUL EXTERIOR RESTORATION

■■ **Priorities:** *Itemize priorities and estimate budgets for each. A disciplined approach gives you a plan that has the best chance of being affordably executed over time. Emergency repairs and structural damage should take precedence over aesthetic and decorative improvements. "We have had to make a lot of agonizing choices about which projects to do and when," says Jane Browne. "We set priorities, we have budgets, and we use alternatives when we need to."*

■■ **Roof Surface:** *Eighty- and ninety-year-old roofs may require extensive repair or replacement. After first sealing the base surface, you may find the original material to be impractical or a new composite material preferable. Monty Montgomery, with a leaking, rotting cedar-shake roof, thought the original shakes were quite beautiful and complemented the shingle siding, but Los Angeles County fire codes prohibit wooden roof surfaces. "I looked at a lot of bungalows in the area," he says, "and visited as many [architect Arthur R.] Kelly houses as I could find, especially his ranch houses." He and Martin Weil came up with an excellent solution: rolled tar paper in a dark charcoal tone, a favorite of Greene & Greene and a popular Arts and Crafts roofing material.*

■■ **Roofline:** *You might be tempted to raise the roofline to add height and useable space to the upper half-story. The Chesters had two small guest rooms upstairs before a tree fell on the roof. "We had always planned to add a full bathroom and increase the guest room's head area and width," says Ms. Chester. "The tree just meant we had to make decisions fast." Thanks to the talent and computerized simulation modeling of alternative rooflines by James Pandula of Blackburn Architects, who had completed the kitchen addition four years earlier, the Chesters doubled the second-floor useable space by raising one hip-roof slope, creating a modified gable to match the front gable, and adding a shed dormer to the rear without altering the scale or stylistic integrity of the Craftsman-style bungalow from the front view.*

■■ **Chimney:** *The bungalow's large living-room fireplaces connect with high chimney stacks containing the flues. Calling in a specialist to inspect the chimney and flues is recommended at least every five years. The chimney's masonry surface, usually brick or stone, may require repointing if water seepage is evident, or the flues may require patching or cleaning, all quite common ailments.*

■■ **Shingle Siding:** *Arts and Crafts shingle siding is part of the bungalow spirit's essence. The Montgomerys meticulously restored the natural cedar shingles to preserve both the natural wood and the appearance of "aged" wood. A shingle refinisher, working for contractor Tim Kelly, replaced original shingles on the front facade that had rotted with original thirteen-foot handcut shingles in good condition from the side and rear facades, and replaced the latter with contemporary three-foot machine-cut shingles. All surfaces were then pressure-washed, bleached, and water-blasted, and now age naturally.*

■■ **Window and Door Glass:** *Old glass has a texture and color that contribute to the windows', and the house's, authentic appearance. Salvage as much of the original glass as possible. To replace broken or cracked panes, the purest and most expensive option is to use authentic wavy glass, which can be purchased for about 50 percent more than pane glass from antique dealers. The Montgomery team, for example, included one individual who traveled the state of California buying old doors and windows that had wavy glass; they threw out the frames once the glass had been salvaged. The second option, which costs about 20 percent more than standard float glass, is to purchase newly made leaded glass, which the Phelpses and Portners have done as needed.*

One of several patio arbors leading out from the Montgomery house. This bungalow melds with the rugged desert terrain to create a truly integrated design of indoor-outdoor living spaces. Landscape architect Sarah Munster regenerated decomposed granite soil and rebuilt much of the stonework surrounding the house and the ten-acre property: landscape crews and college students gathered original stones, and the contractor shipped in twice as much fresh stone from a New Mexico riverbed. The landscape plan evolved as the Montgomerys and Ms. Munster cleared away dead trees and cacti, restoring succulent cacti and vegetation to emphasize natural, monochromatic plant shapes, textures, and foliage. This small arbor leads out from the rear kitchen and a small study (originally the maid's bedroom); stone and packed-dirt terraces appear around the house and the property, opening out from the owner's office, the living room, the kitchen, and the pantry at the rear.

reproduction lamps, sconces, and lighting fixtures throughout the house, adapted from authentic designs;

■ ■ building additional wall closets for storage in the library, the study, and the kitchen, a cabinet design patterned after the mahogany linen cabinet in the upstairs hall;

■ ■ furnishing each room and outdoor living area with antique Mission and Craftsman furnishings, and complementary American Indian textiles and floor coverings;

■ ■ removing the original pergola lining the 10-percent-grade driveway from the base of the property to the entrance to reinforce the eroded site and improve car and pedestrian passage up and down the narrow, steep driveway. In addition, the outer stone walls and the dry-rotted front porch were rebuilt.

The Portner house living room, Chicago. From the large brick fireplace, framed by stained-glass windows in blazing purple tones and glass-fronted built-in cabinets, to the Portners' extensive Roseville Pottery collection acquired over several years, including the Japanese cast-bronze elephants, circa 1910, and the rare 1928 "Futura" Roseville pot upon the mantel, the furnishings and details project an ideal Arts and Crafts sensibility.

THE LIVING ROOM & SITTING NOOK

T HE RESTORATION DESIGN OF THE LIVING ROOM—THE BUNGALOW'S LARGEST ROOM—EVOKES WARMTH, COMFORT, AND OPENNESS. CRAFTSMANSHIP IN the bungalow spirit emphasizes the materials, colors, and textures indigenous to nature. Sitting nooks, usually integrated within the living room as inglenooks, are smaller and cozier spaces, such as those in the Phelps house. They might also be separate libraries or sitting rooms, such as in the Browne, Chester, and Montgomery houses. These quiet spaces of repose feature personal elements of

creative artistry and the craftsman flare of mica floor lamps and reclining Morris chairs, shaded sconces and crackling fireplaces, and colorful art-glass windows over built-in benches.

THE LIVING ROOM

As the center point of the bungalow's open floor plan, the living room's design sets the tone and the stylistic theme for other rooms, whether rustic (Montgomery house), informal (Phelps and Browne houses), or more elegant (Portner and Chester houses). Through years of collecting Arts and Crafts pieces, each owner has created a very personal yet stylized living-room space with old

antiques and new reproductions, acquiring locally and traveling cross-country to antique haunts, flea markets, garage sales, and fine-arts dealers.

Each owner's restoration style stems from personal interpretations of bungalow values today (chapter 1), filtered through personal habits, tastes, and financial resources. These factors define choices about when to purchase and the most realistic alternatives available to achieve the desired results with furnishings, lighting fixtures, wall coverings, textiles, collectibles, and art. If cost is the issue, then alternatives can always be found, perhaps not as pure or perfect, but suitable. "I needed a couch

Monty Montgomery's study is a quiet place next to the library at the rear of the house, leading out to a private patio. It is designed in the restful ambiance of informal Adirondack-style influences, as transparent glazing sheaths the fir wood paneling and the mahogany-stained Douglas fir floor, and the simple Mission-style desk and leather-studded side chair sit neatly in the corner, looking out the window.

that blended with the room's Craftsman and Prairie style," says Jane Browne, "but we weren't willing to spend a small fortune on a Stickley couch, original or reproduction. It also had to be comfortable to sit on." Happily, the Brownes found the right piece in J. C. Penny's Bassett line.

Arts and Crafts lighting fixtures also reflect cost and quality choices. In leaded-art-glass lamps and shades, the Brownes, Portners,

and Phelpses have acquired across the full range of craftsmanship and expense: high-end Tiffany lamps and shades in the Portner, Browne, and Phelps living rooms; very good Peters and Frankl lamps in the Portner living and dining rooms; and moderately good and economical Pittsburgh lamps and shades in selected places in the Portner house.

With each restoration—regardless of whether the owners hired an architect and

The Portner house's original brass sconces (which, after five years of searching, the Portners topped with antique lamp shades) remain, twelve in all around the living room and dining room. The owners discovered seventy-year-old frayed cloth wiring as they restored the living- and dining-room sconces and other fixtures throughout the house. With the expertise of a professional electrician, they incrementally upgraded electrical sockets, fixtures, and wiring over a ten-year period.

contractor (Montgomery and Chester), or worked closely with a local carpenter and other specialists (Browne), or largely executed the work themselves (Phelps), and whether they chose the finest and most expensive options or lower-cost alternatives—the bungalow's original architecture is impeccably restored with full respect for the historic design.

In the Browne, Chester, Portner, and Montgomery houses, the efficient layout of rooms maximizes useable living area and minimizes hall spaces. This begins at the front door, which opens into the living room in each house.

Creating open vistas and generous passages around and into the room emphasizes the living room's central position. This is achieved by furnishing with couches, chairs, and lamps that are low in height, and creating visual and sitting ensembles rather than individual showpieces, such as an exquisite armoire, a Louis XV sofa, or a piece of sculpture. In restoring the comfort and restfulness of Arts and Crafts environments to these living rooms—notably

BEING TRUE TO THE ARTS AND CRAFTS LEGACY

"I adore the smell of sawdust," says Cathy Phelps, *"and I love to create functional spaces and re-create historic houses."* As a restoration designer and space planner, she truly enjoys the restoration process. This talent came to fruition in her own living room as she restored the Craftsman heritage the previous owner had thoroughly Victorianized.

"We used old photographs from the first owner's grandson and the second owners to re-create the living room and dining room as close to the original as possible." In the living room, she and her husband, Lew, salvaged the original oak French doors from storage, refinished them with a natural stain and new glazing, then rehung two sets of double doors in the long wall between living room and porch.

"We also used design references from other parts of the original house to re-create the living room," Cathy adds, *"mostly from the kitchen cabinets and the dining-room sideboard."* She drew on her own craftsmanship, designing the Prairie-style table behind the couch and the Craftsman-style stereo cabinet in the game/music nook.

The Phelpses' fireplace inglenook is a part of the living room, shown here in 1910 with the Lincoln Clark family, the original patrons, clustered around the warm fire. Through diligent and careful research of previous owners, the Phelpses located the grandson of the first owner, Lincoln Clark III, who provided early photographs and remembrances of the living room and dining room for restoration guidance. The central fireplace remained the main source of heat until 1941, when subsequent owners installed central heating.

in the Phelps, Browne, and Montgomery houses—the owners brought together a palette of earth tones, natural fabrics, woods and metals, amber lighting, and simple furniture arrangements.

Indeed, the bungalow's early popularity rose out of a quiet rebellion against the formality of late-nineteenth-century Victorian interiors and their compartmentalized spaces. The incongruity of stuffiness in a Craftsman interior is exactly what jarred the Phelpses when they first walked into their unrestored house. The Brownes and Montgomerys have enhanced unobstructed sight lines and the rooms' linear designs with low-backed furniture pieces and focal points around doorways, including planters, wall hangings, bookcases,

chairs and benches, color changes on walls, and textiles. The Portners had only to clean the double French doors between the living room and dining room, leaving them unshaded to act as tranparent oak and mahogany veils between the rooms.

THE FIREPLACE

Henry Saylor's popular 1911 pattern book, *Bungalows: Their Design, Construction and Furnishing,* preached that the fireplace is the bungalow's symbolic center, its raison d'être: "a bungalow without a fireplace" is like "a garden without flowers." Indeed, the living room centers around the fireplace as an expression of hospitality with family and friends. For California bungalows, the fireplace remained the singular heating source through the first half of the century, until later homeowners began to install central heating.

Low and broad, the fireplace is either an integral feature within the living area (as in the Montgomery, Chester, Portner, and Browne houses), or set apart within the room as a cozy inglenook (the Phelps house). In some bungalows, a higher or lower floor level, or a lower ceiling height, separates the inglenook from the main room. Built-in wooden benches with cushioned seats commonly frame either side or the front of the fireplace, as in the Phelps house, especially in California bungalows and those styled in the Craftsman manner.

Built-in bookcases flanking the hearth, often with small art-glass windows above, are one of the finest and most common features. In the Portner house, for example, the fireplace and bookcases with leaded-glass windows above span the full end of the room, providing the stylistic focal point for furnishing this room. The leaded glass, in a colorful floral design, also appears in a complementary design in the vestibule and front entrance windows. (Previous owners removed and walled over the Chester house's original bookcases with square leaded-glass windows above.)

WINDOWS

Groups of casements, large picture windows, French doors, and banks of small Craftsman windows link the interior with nature and admit streams of natural light and fresh air, amplifying the sense of space and the continuity with adjacent rooms. Standing in the middle of the Phelps or Chester or Montgomery living rooms, one is surrounded by nature's colors, and the sights and sounds of animated activity outside spill through open windows.

Certainly bungalows located in southern

RESTORED ENTRANCES FOR COMMUNAL LIVING

■■ *The **Montgomerys'** heavy, oversized mahogany front door leads into a small stairhall, then the spacious living room to the left and the small library to the right. To restore the original 1910 Craftsman-style hanging lamp that illuminated the front door and porch, contractor Tim Kelly carefully dismantled the old lamp, refinished the wood, and replaced the golden art glass, then cleaned the brass chain. He took great care in restoring the massive wood door and three-over-three small windows, one etched with the architect's initials. For convenience, a Mission Revival-style reproduction table stands in the stairhall, the household drop-off place for keys, sunglasses, and messages.*

■■ *The **Portner** entrance presents a succession of connecting spaces, from the front porch outside, into the enclosed vestibule to buffer cold-air drafts gusting into the living room (furnished with an umbrella stand and small glove table), then to the hallway that opens into the living room. In the hall, the Portners had only to clean the colorful art-glass windows, refinish and stain the oak floors and mahogany trim, and furnish with a period-style coat tree, side table, and mohair chaise lounge.*

■■ *The **Chester** and **Phelps** entrance thresholds open directly into the living room, on axis with the large fireplace, the heart of the home. With entrance mats inside the doors, the owners created restoration designs that turned toward the rooms' centers, around the fireplace.*

Cathy Phelps, an interior designer, designed this Craftsman-style stereo chest for the wall space in the living room's adjacent music/reading nook. Created in the early 1990s "to look like it was built for the house," she says, it repeats details found elsewhere in house furnishings of the chest's design, including the dining-room-furniture peg motif and the geometric pattern of two narrow panels over a large panel for window panes and built-in cabinets.

California, and the Mid-Atlantic and southern states, with temperate climates and sunshine eight months of the year, enjoy longer daylight hours, while bungalows in Chicago and the midwestern states are limited to less than six spring and summer months. The Phelpses, Brownes, and Montgomerys, following popular Craftsman and Mission styles, enhance the effect of light and air by leaving windows uncurtained and unpainted, and refinishing the fine wood trim with a natural matte finish. In the Chester living room, with neocolonial influences dominating the interior, sheer and simple curtains dress the windows, while other ground-floor rooms are curtainless to enhance the bungalow's wooden details.

Southern and eastern exposures, always recommended in residential design, remain a

In the Portners' Chicago living room, the corner between the mohair sofa and the built-in window seat offers an ideal sitting nook for reading or for watching passersby through the picture window. The 1920s Peters lamp, similar to art-glass lamps in the Arts and Crafts genre, portrays a highly detailed scene of nature in the leaded-glass shade and the welded-brass base.

STRIPPING PAINT IN ONE EASY STEP: CALL AN EXPERT

White enamel paint covered the Brownes' fine oak windows when they bought the house. "I thought I could strip and refinish them myself," says Jane Browne. "How hard could it be?"

One living-room window took her over a month. With fourteen windows in the living room alone and another twelve on the ground floor, she wisely called in her expert carpenter and refinisher, Tony Aducci, who knows wood, paint, and the chemical formulas to use for stripping and refinishing. Tony completed the job in less than a month.

primary goal of Arts and Crafts designers so that maximum sunlight can reflect against the honey and earth tones of wood and fabrics. The Montgomery house literally basks in the warm glow of architect Authur Kelly's Feng Shui siting, with the living room facing south, the dining room and kitchen facing east, and the second-floor master bedroom and sleeping porch facing east and south; uncurtained windows soak in the natural light.

At dusk and during the night, rooms turn to an amber hue with the low, mica-shaded lights reflecting off the honey-toned oak in the Montgomery, Browne, and Phelps houses. Bright illumination, perhaps desirable in the context of contemporary fluorescent lighting standards, is less appropriate in a period restoration.

WOODWORK

Restored living-room woodwork ideally is stripped of paint (a time-consuming job) and naturally stained, varnished, or shellacked. The original finish should be reapplied during restoration by the owner or a professional wood refinisher. Different from neocolonial and Victorian designs, which achieve dramatic room colors with deep-toned paints on woodwork, bungalow restoration design, as created by the Brownes, Montgomerys, Phelpses, and Portners, infuses color and textures through the choice of furniture, textiles, fireplace tiles, wall friezes, stenciling or patterned wallpapers, oriental rugs, pottery, leaded-glass lamps, and art-glass windows.

The natural horizontal running boards in the Montgomery's mahogany-paneled ceiling produce a strong visual flow through the room and a grounded low-lying ambiance. No paint color or wallpaper is needed; the woodwork's structural pattern provides the decorative theme. In contrast to flat, horizontal boards, a box-beam ceiling pattern tends to close in the living room's spaciousness and should be

The Portners' eclectic Arts and Crafts-style living room is dominated by the central brick fireplace and natural mahogany wood trim (with original stain), set against the lighter ochre paint on walls and the purple and crimson hues of the 1920s Chinese deco rug and mohair sofa and chairs. Naturally stained oak floors run through the house.

At the heart of the Chester house, the living room flows easily into adjacent rooms, yet each area appears distinct: the wide opening into the dining room, right; the open portal with broken pedimented trim into the kitchen, upper right; the large master bedroom facing to the rear of the house, upper left; and the small sitting room (originally one of two bedrooms), left. The battered, or sloping, brick fireplace is an upgraded feature in this authentic Sears mail-order bungalow.

In keeping with the architect's intent to create a serene living environment, the Montgomerys painstakingly restored the aged patina in this Mission Revival interior, using period-appropriate techniques and materials throughout. In the living room, horizontal-running ceiling panels emphasize the room's low-lying grounding. Dark-stained bookcases to either side of the doorway openings at both ends emphasize the room's breadth, re-created from the original architect's drawings and early photographs. A hardwood oak floor resonates a honey-oak tone, echoed in the tanned-leather sofa and chairs, original burlap wall coverings, and the prominent brick fireplace. Authentic Craftsman-style pieces include the bird's-eye-maple reading chair, *left background,* acquired from the Roycroft Inn's Ralph Waldo Emerson Suite, and the rustic wooden Roycroft bench from the Roycroft Inn, complemented by colorful Mission Revival-style influences in the scattered, double-weave, American Indian rugs, cushions, and blankets acquired over fifteen years with the New York antiques firm of Kelter Malce. The restoration design was executed by Los Angeles architect Eli Martin Weil, furniture curator and Arts and Crafts designer Roger L. Conant Williams, and contractor Tim Kelly.

The southern California light floods the Phelpses' living room from south-facing porch, left, and west-facing piano nook, center. The restoration encompasses Craftsman-style French doors leading out to the south-facing porch, and grass-cloth wall covering in a golden ochre, chosen to be sympathetic yet lighter than the original 1908 mahogany brown grass cloth. The generic Craftsman-style chair and lamp, *left,* complement the authentic Stickley clipped-end side table and footstool, right. The leaded-glass Handel lamp and Handel shade, rear corner, are two separate pieces collected by the owners; the coffee table is a contemporary Ethan Allen piece, supplementing the absence of coffee tables in original Craftsman interiors, when couches and chairs were arranged for reading and talking in groups, not for lounging and leisure as they often are today. Couches draped in natural canvas and the Sarouk oriental rug enhance authentic furnishings.

used sparingly, more often in dining-room design, as in the Browne house.

LIGHTING

The light in these bungalows, all occupied by avid readers, is sufficient during daylight hours, especially on sunny days. The greater challenge for many of these Craftsman- or Mission-style bungalows is providing adequate and correct artificial lighting after sunset and before sunrise. The tawny light given off by mica and leaded-glass lamp shades, and even fireplaces, is designed to lend the ambient warmth of the Arts and Crafts genre. These houses follow period-style design, and all are lighted with Craftsman-style fixtures in the principal living and dining rooms.

This does indeed limit the room's light levels and betrays our contemporary expectation about bright white light. Yet white light in the living room and dining room especially is inconsistent and unsympathetic with the Arts and Crafts bungalow vernacular. The choice is a personal one. One alternative is to read in a room other than the living or dining room; another is to position bright reading spotlights next to particular chairs or sitting areas.

The Brownes have created Craftsman-style corners such as this one throughout the house with pieces collected over the years, such as the "X"-motif oak desk, found at a Sandwich, Illinois, summer fair.

REFINISHING WOODWORK MAY NOT BE A FIRST PRIORITY . . .

The mahogany trim in the Portners' living room is finished with the original shellac, which, over almost eight decades, has acquired a "crocodile" effect, a cracking in a leather-like pattern. The wood is in excellent condition, though the Portners would eventually like to refinish it, remove the old shellac, and replace it with new, as appropriate.

They asked a restoration craftsperson and an expert wood refinisher to inspect the wood, and each recommended an application that re-creates the transparent color, texture, and luster of the historic finish while enhancing the trim's durability and aesthetic appearance. Because it is not an immediate hazard to the historic character or the condition of the woodwork, Felicia Portner says, "I would love to do it, but I am not quite ready to spend the money" on such an expensive project. It remains at the forefront of her mind and on the long-term "to do" list.

The dark-stained walnut trim around the windows and doors in the Chester house's front sitting room, originally a bedroom, highlights the significance of wood crafts and artistic trim to bungalow design.

RESTORATION-STYLE LIVING ROOMS

Each owner has made choices in developing a restoration style. They emphasize certain elements in the living room, with personal choices based on taste and living habits, and stylistic choices stemming from the spirit, scale, and craft of the original architecture.

BROWNE HOUSE, CHICAGO, ILLINOIS
CRAFTSMAN- AND PRAIRIE-STYLE
LIVING ROOM

■■ **Nature's colors** are infused throughout the room in wall paint and paper, fireplace and table-top accents, and furniture woods and fabrics. Amber lighting emphasizes the richness of the earth tones (brown and moss green), wood (natural oak), light (bright sun and auburn yellow), and fire (burnt sienna reds, purples, and oranges).

■■ **Theme motifs** define personal restoration style, repeated from room to room to express point of view and establish visual continuity: candlesticks, Roycroft artists' works, "X" symbol in furniture, flowers and plants (i.e., the rose, the gingko leaf, potted narcissus), Frank Lloyd Wright ceramic designs, and books all around.

■■ **Genuine artisan crafts** on walls and in textiles, chairs, rugs, ceramics, prints, and art

Impeccable Craftsman-style furnishings and accessories bring comfort and cozy sitting nooks into the Browne house's spacious living room. French doors, removed by the previous owner, originally separated the south-facing front porch from the living-room space; integrated, the band of windows pulls natural light through the room to reflect off the mocha-brown painted walls (Benjamin Moore), bordered by an Arts and Crafts-reproduction border paper ("Historic Homes Book No. 4"). The owner stripped and cleaned decades of paint buildup from windows, assisted by a loyal local carpenter, and refinished the original oak hardwood floors with natural stain. Early-twentieth-century wicker chairs mix with the generic Morris-style rocker, armchairs, and footstools, circa 1910. The "X" motif in the desk, *upper right,* is a personal favorite that the owner has found in several antique acquisitions. The makeshift Craftsman-style coffee table is actually an authentic, modified Craftsman library table, and the comfortable sofa is a reproduction piece from J. C. Penny's "Bassett" line of furniture.

This Stickley leather-covered reclining chair and mica floor lamp invite fireside reading and napping. Nature's influences are all around: in the brick hearth painted moss green, the dry-weed pedestal by Oak Park artist Robert Munman, *left,* and the burlap antimacassar embroidered in the popular Arts and Crafts gingko-leaf pattern. The fireplace andirons are authentic pieces purchased for five dollars at a local garage sale.

Rich burnt-red walls (Sherwin Williams, Roycroft collection) bordered by reproduction "Thornberry" paper (Bradbury & Bradbury), and the generic oak desk carved after nature's image exemplify the Arts and Crafts spirit in the Brownes' small den, originally a bedroom adjacent to the bathroom on one side and the kitchen on the other. The antique time-card clock, *rear left,* accents the Craftsman-style reproduction pieces to create a sitting room of contemporary comfort and authentic Arts and Crafts detail: a new couch adapted from an original Stickley design; contemporary Craftsman- and Prairie-style oak radiator covers designed and built for the owner by Berwyn, Illinois, carpenter Tony Aducci; and mica lamp shades by artist Louis Glesmann over discount-store brass bases.

glass solidify the Arts and Crafts spirit, including the one-of-a-kind screen designed by Paul Kramer, who tanned the leather and fumed the quarter-oak wood; the tall and slender carved weed holders by Robert Munman, Oak Park; the fireplace-mantel print by Roycroft artist Kathleen West; the embroidered burlap antimacassar over the back of the Stickley reclining chair; and the mica-shaded Craftsman- and Prairie-style lamps by Louis Glesmann and Stewart Surfer of Craftsman Footsteps.

▪▪ **Arts and Crafts furnishings** establish a comfortable ambiance, designed in Craftsman oak, Arts and Crafts wicker, and Morris-style oak and leather; authentic pieces mixed with a few contemporary adaptations improve comfort and reduce costs.

▪▪ **Naturally stained window trim** strongly influences the Craftsman-style design; previously painted windows with light-toned enamel effectively closed in the room, lacking the simple and honest spirit of natural oak.

CHESTER HOUSE, WASHINGTON, D.C.
CRAFTSMAN AND
COLONIAL REVIVAL STYLES

▪▪ The living room's **southern exposure and light-filled ambiance** amplify the room's actual space, which is actually modest in area (13 feet wide by 21 feet long).

▪▪ The **neoclassical broken pediment** walnut trim, highlighted in dark stain against ivory painted walls, formalizes the design standard of this rather simple bungalow with conventional neoclassic detail, greatly upgrading the overall interior for minimal cost.

▪▪ Arts and Crafts **ceiling beams,** running the width of the room, emphasize breadth and spatial flow.

▪▪ **The communal front porch,** opening into the living room, is sheathed in warm tones of beige and forest green; the front living room's **cozy inglenook ambiance** establishes the

house's bungalow spirit, with the prominent fireplace on axis with the entrance door, connecting home with hearth and reinforcing the communal living environment. Drawing on this domestic program, the kitchen/breakfast nook/porch renovation and addition opens the living space to the surrounding landscape.

▪▪ Respecting the **openness with other rooms** (dining room, kitchen, bedroom, and sitting room), furniture faces the center, and doorway portals are free of obstruction.

PHELPS HOUSE, PASADENA, CALIFORNIA
CRAFTSMAN STYLE

▪▪ Distinct **seating areas** in this Craftsman-style living room create a truly functional family room for evening philosophizing, individual reading, group game playing, and piano practice. The fireplace nook, openly integrated into the larger living room, encourages social interchange while separating functions and affording a quiet area if desired. The music/game/stereo nook provides an area for separate activity, a generously windowed space that is light-filled during the day and cozily lit at night.

▪▪ **Windows all around**—casements, French doors, and double-hung windows—flood the room with the southern California light to create a true California bungalow spirit.

▪▪ An open **porch connection** through the restored Craftsman French doors integrates interior living space with outdoor living space amid the open landscape, and maximizes the impact of the living room and rear porch's southern exposure.

▪▪ **Air circulation** enhances the indoor-outdoor integration and the sense of openness within the room and throughout the house, with fresh breezes wafting through groups of open windows and out the porch's French doors as well as across the house's breadth through the operable leaded-glass windows framing the inglenook and into the separate rear hallway.

■ ■ **Natural fabrics and wall coverings** reinforce the California bungalow and Craftsman spirit: the natural, canvas-upholstered contemporary furniture, the period-style grass-cloth wall covering, the authentic Turkish Sarouk rug, and the William Morris textile all mix with simple oak chairs, tables, and cabinets.

PORTNER HOUSE, CHICAGO, ILLINOIS
ARTS & CRAFTS STYLE

■ ■ The fine, **eclectic mix of early-twentieth-century Arts and Crafts** furnishings, textiles, rugs, and accessories, crafted in silks, wools, velveteens, rich colors, and darker woods, lends an elegant and formal ambiance to this bungalow living room.

■ ■ An extensive collection of **authentic Arts and Crafts antique pieces**—including the Roseville Pottery, the Frankl and Peters art-glass shades and pot-metal lamps, the Chinese deco rug, the mohair couch and chairs, the original shaded sconces, and the ironwork deco tables—combine to filter a solid Arts and Crafts style through every detail.

■ ■ Naturally stained floors and wood trim emphasize the bungalow's **woodenness.**

■ ■ **Strong colors complementing one another**—deep reds, purples, golds, greens, and blues—offer a bright alternative to the muted, natural tones in the Craftsman- and Mission-style restoration designs of the Browne and Montgomery houses.

■ ■ The restoration design emphasizes the **art display:** the design and craft of the Roseville Pottery, the leaded-glass lamp shade and windows, the iron sculptures and sconces, and the deep colors of glass and textiles. The number of furniture pieces are minimized, taking advantage of built-in benches and cabinets.

MONTGOMERY HOUSE,
HOLLYWOOD, CALIFORNIA
MISSION STYLE

■ ■ The **natural aged patina of the oak, fir, and** cedar structure establishes the foundation of the rustic and honey-toned restoration design. The rustic is expressed through unadorned natural windows, the burlap wall covering, the American Indian textiles, the original Roycroft Inn log bench, the Stickley leather chair, and the tanned-leather couch and chairs.

■ ■ The room's **natural and artificial lighting** offers contrasts by day and night: the brilliant southern sun streams in through large window areas dawn to dusk, and mica-shaded lamps and lighting fixtures reproduced in adaptation Stickley designs by Michael Adams warm the large room with a soft amber hue during evening hours and rainy afternoons. **Lamps and lighting fixtures** are exclusively period style, including Craftsman mica-shaded lamps and iron-gridded lanterns.

■ ■ The original **linear design,** from doorway to doorway, is emphasized by the restored, dark-stained horizontal ceiling beams and the rebuilt bookcases to either side of the open portals at each end, literally providing book-ends to define the parameters and direct the spatial flow of the long room.

■ ■ **Openness** is amplified by the **low-rise furniture,** the continuity of the honey-toned oak floor, and the scattered placement of colorful, rectangular, American Indian rugs.

■ ■ The **Feng Shui** theory of yin and yang and the five elements guided the architect's original design and the owner's restoration, with emphasis on avoiding straight lines and sharp points throughout and between rooms, and opening spaces and keeping rooms and doorways free of obstructions to allow chi, or powerful heavenly energies, to flow and settle freely. The architect's originally designed sun exposures are enhanced by open and unadorned windows, the honey-toned stain of oak floors and trim to absorb light, and the ivory enamel paint in kitchen, pantry, bedrooms, and library to reflect light.

The Montgomery house dining room, set at a wide angle to the living room to conform with the curving hillside, mixes Mission Revival and Craftsman styling in natural and amber tones with an unvarnished ambiance set by the unpainted brick fireplace and oak-paneled walls, which rise to the height of the plate rail, and the wall space above covered with golden burlap, which blends with the living room through the wide opening. The plain, Mission-style chestnut dining table and oak leather-back chairs complement the original Stickley oak ladder-back chairs and the reproduction Stickley lamp design by Michael Adams, New York. Patron C. L. Frost commissioned the California plein-air painting, associated with the Arts and Crafts movement, for the wall above the fireplace mantel when he built the house. Monty Montgomery bought the piece from Kate Frost Tufts in 1993 and hopes it will always stay with the bungalow.

THE DINING ROOM & THE KITCHEN

THE RESTORATION DESIGN OF THE DINING ROOM, AS AN EXTENSION OF THE LIVING ROOM, INTEGRATES ONE WITH THE OTHER IN A COMPLEMENTARY manner. The dining room is crafted to achieve the ambiance of domesticity as well as elegance, for this is probably the most formal room in the house. In many bungalows, the dining room opens into a sunroom of wood-trimmed windows and summer screens on all sides. A cozy, enclosed library where the family retires at the end of the day may also adjoin the dining room. ▪▪ Adjacent to the dining

room, the kitchen opens through a swinging door, a short utility hallway, or a small pantry. The bungalow kitchen, in contrast with contemporary kitchens that interweave with the dining room and family room, is an enclosed and separate space, a design feature that originated in the early 1900s as a means to ensure cleanliness in food preparation and containment of unappealing scenes. The restoration-style kitchen adheres to a minimalist design, respecting Arts and Crafts designers' heightened consciousness about the primacy of sanitary and efficient work spaces in the kitchen's domain.

THE DINING ROOM

More than any other room, the dining room is designed to achieve a harmonious mix of color, texture, and materials on surfaces and furniture. The restoration of these bungalow dining rooms carefully respects Arts and Crafts design by placing the focus on the contextual scene of walls and ceiling—the architectural borderland—rather than the singular dining table at center. Dining-room restoration design balances the *architecture*, the *built-in features*, and the *moveable furniture*. The goal is to achieve an ensemble among these three elements, the mix of which might be adjusted for features that cannot be altered or moved, such as the room's architecture (dimensions or light orientation), existing alterations by earlier owners (removal of paneling or ceiling beams), or the lack of built-in furniture.

ARCHITECTURAL FEATURES

The architecture of the room tends to be *roughly square*, either a perfect square or a broad rectangle, integrated with the living-room area through a wide opening. *French doors or sliding pocket doors* are typical features separating the two rooms, even though the doors often remain open and each room is considered a continuation of the other in design and function. The naturally stained wood of the French or pocket doors matches the wood of the room into which it faces. The oak French doors between living and dining room in the Portner house, for example, are naturally stained oak facing the living room and a darker, mahogany-stained veneer facing the mahogany-paneled dining room. *Ceiling beams* and *paneling* also differentiate the dining-room and living-room areas, such as in the Montgomery and Chester houses.

In the Montgomery house, the oak ceiling panels flow horizontally across the long living room to the threshold of the small dining room, where the paneling runs perpendicular to the living-room ceiling, east to west, in keeping with the Feng Shui philosophy of home design and healthful living that architect Arthur Kelly applied in this house design. In the Browne dining room, the owners added the corner box-beam ceiling motif to enhance the effect of this smaller room's cozy domesticity and to contrast it with the long and spacious living room. The coordinated Craftsman-style oak trim amplifies the room's architecture, including the box ceil-

The Brownes found this small sideboard buffet at an antique fair in Madison, Wisconsin, a generic period piece, circa 1910, with a Queen Anne-style splashboard (a reference to an earlier era of Victorian design, which is common in later pieces) and Arts and Crafts-style brass drawer pulls in a strong ring geometry. The owners added the plate rail in the mid-1990s, working with designer Paul Duchscherer and carpenter Tony Aducci. The buffet stands against the facing wall between dining room and living room, *left*, the wide opening giving the sense that the rooms are part of one another.

ing, plate rail, and wall paneling, a coordinated design the Brownes created in collaboration with San Francisco designer Paul Duchscherer and local carpenter Tony Aducci.

High-paneled wainscoting in naturally stained oak, pine, or walnut is another period-style architectural feature in bungalow dining rooms. The wainscoting in Arts and Crafts interiors, particularly those designed in the Craftsman and Tudor Revival styles, rises to the height of the plate rail, about two feet below the ceiling, with the bordering frieze encircling the room. Together, the *ceiling beams*, *plate rails*, and *high-paneled wainscoting* enhance the dining room's woodenness, as in the Browne, Phelps, Portner, and Montgomery houses.

MIRRORS ENLARGE AND BRIGHTEN

Mirrors are a period-style design technique especially common in dining-room sideboards and on walls, adding to the sense of openness and the play of light through windows and across rooms.

A place setting in the Browne dining room mixes English Arts and Crafts china bowls, *center,* with well-chosen complementary dishes from discount outlets T.J. Maxx and Cost Plus. The hand-embroidered linen napkin and table scarf, stenciled in nature's themes of the pinecone and American beauty rose, respectively, are adapted from a circa 1910 design and recreated by Dianne Ayres Arts and Crafts Period Textiles.

The built-in sideboard is the centerpiece of the Phelpses' dining-room restoration design, complementing the architecture of the California bungalow and guiding the selection of furnishings to create the room's Craftsman-style ensemble. They refinished this piece with a matte natural stain as a conservation measure.

The wainscot paneling may be solid wood (Portner and Montgomery houses) or vertical strips of wood spaced about every fourteen inches to create the effect of wall panels; paper, paint, or stenciled scenes cover the wall surface (Browne house). Between ceiling and wainscoting, the wide decorative frieze often appears as the room's most colorful element, the encircling border covered with tapestried wallpaper or applied stenciling in muted natural tones of olive yellow, forest green, or earth brown, as in the Browne and Phelps houses.

Arts and Crafts designers also recommend border motifs of nature's landscapes, leaves, flowers, gingko trees, and, occasionally, animals to enliven the dining room's decor. The wallpapered or stenciled frieze became quite popular in early bungalow houses, especially Craftsman-style interiors, for in these modest-sized rooms, the decorative frieze offered substantial impact for modest cost. For the bungalows featured here, the owners chose a simpler unadorned frieze to complement the room's more animated elements of deep color tones, texture, furniture, and crafted wood trim to create a more subdued and muted aura in the overall room ensemble. On wall and ceiling surfaces, warm and muted earth tones complement the deeper tones of the wood trim, as in the Browne house, with paneled walls below the plate rail painted a low-toned moss green and the frieze above a light ocher shade. The goal is to avoid sharp contrasts in color, especially between the natural wood and the applied decor of wall and ceiling surfaces.

BUILT-IN FEATURES

The *built-in features* reinforce the aesthetic value of both the architectural design and the moveable furniture. The dining room's main built-in piece is the naturally stained sideboard buffet, with or without a mirror to enhance the room's spaciousness (an antique mirror might

The Brownes' Craftsman-style restoration design is created by the oak wall paneling, designed by Paul Duchscherer and carpenter Tony Aducci, who extended naturally stained vertical strips (spaced about every fourteen inches) from the plate rail (the horizontal wood molding twenty-two inches below the ceiling) to the floor molding. The wainscoting's moss green paint complements the lighter green of the frieze; the light beige on the ceiling offsets the oak box-beam ceiling (Sherwin Williams Roycroft collection paints). A claw-footed Queen Anne table, vintage late nineteenth century, could be found in many bungalow dining rooms, even though an imperfect detail. The owner found the 1910 Craftsman chairs by Fore Johnson, part of Stickley's furniture line, through an antiques dealer, while the generic oak sideboard, *right,* came from the Sandwich, Illinois, antiques fair.

The Chester house offers a perfect solution to the integration of dining room and living room with this high-walled, open, broken-pedimented portal, providing a visual connection and easy flow while also a clear separation of spaces.

Reproduction Roycroft dishware, from the Roycroft Shops in East Aurora, New York, fills the glass-fronted cabinets in the Montgomery pantry.

The built-in sideboard, crafted with brass drawer pulls and structural pegs that are part of the ornament, informed the Phelpses in selecting their Craftsman-style square oak table, with its prominent pegs at structural joints, and authentic H-backed Stickley chairs, acquired from Pasadena antiques dealers Ricky Kersey and Michele Sekula. To restore the original plate rail previous owners had removed when modernizing the dining room to 1970s standards, the Phelpses retained restoration architect William Ellinger to interpret 1940s photographs taken by the second owners, showing the original plate rail. The restored rail is a prominent element in the Arts and Crafts design of this dining room, used for displaying Arts and Crafts collections of china, silver, brass, and pottery.

be scarred or damaged and require professional restoration). Glass-doored cabinets and window seats also appear as traditional dining-room built-ins. In many Craftsman-style dining rooms, the large built-in buffet occupying one full wall enjoyed wide appeal, such as in the Phelps house, enhanced here by the glass-fronted cabinets to either side and leaded casement windows above, an artistic feature that also has the practical purpose of improving air circulation in this hot California climate. Glass-fronted built-in cabinets originally framed the broad doorway leading into the Portner dining room, as evidenced by the architect's 1922 drawings, a feature the owners re-created by acquiring and placing early-twentieth-century china chests to either side of the opening.

FURNITURE

Completing the Arts and Crafts-style dining-room ensemble, *furniture* harmonizes with the built-ins and the room's architectural design. Table, chairs, sideboards, and period-style china, pottery, and textiles (upholstery, table scarf, rug, and window curtains), col-

Built-in glass-fronted cabinets, painted a washable and bright ivory enamel, frame the Montgomerys' pantry, a small room between the kitchen and the dining room leading out to a rear terrace. The draft cold-storage chest, an authentic period piece, has been refitted inside as an electric refrigerator, though smaller than contemporary standards.

lected from a variety of local and out-of-state antiques dealers, furniture fairs, garage sales, and newspaper ads, respect the vision established by the architecture and the built-ins. The *major pieces* typically include the *sideboard buffet*, which can be a moveable piece acquired by the owner, and the *dining-room table*, naturally stained and, ideally, designed in a manner that complements or matches the sideboard (as in the Phelps house). The Phelpses' Craftsman-style Stickley table, which they acquired when they restored this room, repeats the sideboard's "pegged" motif in the legs.

THE KITCHEN

If strictly interpreted, the restoration-style bungalow kitchen would reflect its early-twentieth-century origins as the exclusive domain of females, either "housewives" or "maids." Yet dramatic social and technological changes, as well as the kitchen's multipurpose domestic role as a family room, strongly influence restoration design decisions today. Certainly these are chief among the reasons many period kitchens have been dismantled and/or not restored. Of the five bungalow houses featured

RESTORATION DESIGN CHOICES

The most successful restoration designs join naturally crafted elements of the structure with stylistic elements of the interior design in a balanced ensemble—Craftsman, Mission, Colonial Revival, etc. Individual parts to consider in planning a restoration design include the following:

■ ■ *high-paneled wainscoting and plate rail (the Browne and Phelps houses);*

■ ■ *wall and ceiling finishes, whether paint, wallpaper, or stenciling (the Montgomery house);*

■ ■ *built-in sideboards and glass-fronted cabinets, beautifully stained and never painted (the Phelps house);*

■ ■ *ceiling beams and cornices, and original wall sconces and hanging lamps (the Portner house);*

■ ■ *dining-room table and chairs. While centrally placed and major handcrafted pieces of wood, they remain supporting elements in defining the room's ensemble (Chester and Browne houses).*

The Portner dining room echoes the overall design style of the house and mixes Arts and Crafts pieces of different, early-twentieth-century influences—medieval Moorish Revival, Craftsman, Chinese deco, and early Nouveau styles. The Chester house, uniformly styled in the Colonial Revival genre, features neoclassical and medieval Moorish influences.

The mahogany-paneled Portner dining room radiates Arts and Crafts elegance. Leading in from the living room, wide French doors open to the Tudor Revival-inspired dark oak table, from the estate sale of a turn-of-the-century Lake Michigan mansion; the chairs are chosen for the softer upholstered seats and sympathetic Jacobean-style legs, rather than the table's heavier, matching leather-back chairs, stored in the basement. The polished-brass, four-lamp chandelier, an adaptation of the Raymond four-light hanging lamp, is designed in the room's Edwardian spirit. The cobalt blue deco pots, *left,* by the Monmouth studio for motion-picture theater lobbies of the 1930s, are a brilliant complement to the 1930s Chinese deco rug.

The Colonial Revival-style architecture of the Chester house inspires eclectic furnishings, such as the Arts and Crafts-style table and sideboard. This bright room receives natural light from the south-facing front and the east-facing side, as well as through the open living room and kitchen areas. The naturally stained heart-pine floor and dark-stained walnut trim are softly contrasted with ivory-painted walls.

The Phelpses' dining room demonstrates the perfection achieved after detailed research and diligent collecting of Craftsman-style pieces. The focal point is the large built-in buffet occupying the room's end, framed by leaded-glass cabinets to either side and beveled-glass casement windows above. Fresh air and eastern light stream in. The large French doors, *right,* which the Phelpses recovered and restored from storage, open to the sunporch and terrace to integrate interior living with nature in the finest Craftsman and California bungalow style. Recollections and photographs from the patron's grandson, Lincoln Clark III, informed the Phelpses' restoration of the plate rail (removed by a previous owner) and the mustard-toned grass-cloth wall covering.

here, three include restored or renovated kitchens (Chester, Montgomery, and Browne), one intact 1910s kitchen that requires restoration (Phelps), and one that has been substantially updated in a nondistinctive style that is not entirely sympathetic with restoration design (Portner).

Contemporary restoration designs respect the bungalow ideals of efficiency, healthfulness, and brightness, while also incorporating dramatically different uses and technologies as well as the presence of multiple functions in the contemporary kitchen. To achieve this domestic program, the bungalow values of simplicity in design and in detail are honed to a sharp focus. Undecorated and unornamented surfaces, with cabinets painted white or ivory enamel and floors of white or white-and-black ceramic tiles, sanded pine, or a light-toned linoleum, ensure ease in washability and cleanliness in cooking. These design elements create the most healthful work environment. In addition, an efficient space plan equipped with conveniences to save steps and make housework more pleasant incorporates the full complement of built-in cabinets and counters. Smaller than the Victorian-era kitchen, the bungalow kitchen features space-saving built-ins rather than free-standing tables and armoires. The emergence of the mechanized kitchen during the bungalow's heyday further refined efficient and healthful design, introducing stove hoods to funnel out cooking smoke, draft coolers for perishable food storage (refrigerators by contemporary standards), built-in flour bins and breadboards, and built-in storage cabinets as part of the bungalow's architecture. Electric appliances appeared in later bungalows of the 1920s and 1930s.

Restoration design today also reflects major changes in the domestic role of the American kitchen: cooking as a social activity often involving more than one person, female

The Phelps house's original kitchen, shown here with Mrs. Lincoln Clark, the first owner, working at the counter with the built-in, glass-fronted cabinets above. To Mrs. Clark's right, the east-facing window above the kitchen sink is a conscious design choice to bring abundant natural light into this plainest of enamel-white rooms.

and male. In this way, restoration design seeks to balance the historic integrity of spatial containment in the bungalow kitchen—principally achieved by doorways fitted with solid wood doors rather than wide portals having transparent French doors—against contemporary demands for spatial openness, internally and with other rooms, to accommodate the kitchen's central social role, principally achieved by open sight lines and swinging doors between the kitchen, dining room, and other rooms.

The restoration-style kitchen can encompass a small breakfast nook (Chester house); a utility porch, known as a mud room in contemporary terms (Chester and Montgomery houses); and a pantry with built-in dresser, drawers, and cupboards (Montgomery house), often located between the kitchen and dining room.

The most successful kitchen renovations achieve a modest no-frills restraint in design, color, and details, offering a kitchen of contemporary standards designed in the period style consistent with the house's interior, and an overall sensibility that respects the values and spirit of the early-twentieth-century bungalow. Sympathetic with bungalow period designs, built-in wooden cabinets, cupboards, and drawers express the linear lines of the wooden carpentry, and plain white or ivory enamel painted walls offer maximum washability and brightness in the natural light. Casement windows above the sink and the principal counter area produce the intended cheery work environment of period designs and also enhance the sense of space, as in the Montgomery and Chester houses.

RESTORATION-STYLE DINING ROOMS AND KITCHENS

For some homeowners, the time and expense of a dining-room restoration takes precedence over creating a period-style kitchen. For those whose domestic life centers around informal entertaining and the kitchen, the focus is on the restoration styling of the kitchen. Personal choices about how the kitchen and dining room are used each day guide restoration decisions.

PHELPS HOUSE, PASADENA, CALIFORNIA CRAFTSMAN STYLE

■ ■ Muted golden ochre **grass-cloth wall covering** diffuses an amber hue through the room during daylight and a soft warmth at night. Sympathetic with the original dark yellow grass cloth, the wall covering is restored in a lighter palette.

■ ■ Diligent research led to the first owner's grandson, Lincoln Clark III, who provided

WHEN TO CALL AN ELECTRICIAN FOR REWIRING

"I wanted to do it myself," says Frank Portner, "but I finally gave in after we had blown three fuses and the lamp still didn't work." When the Portners began restoring the dining-room sconces and hanging lamp, they discovered frayed and crumbling wiring that literally was too hot for them to repair on their own. At first reluctant to bring in a professional electrician, mostly because of time and expense, they relented when circuits shorted and sparks flew as they attempted to repair sockets and outlets.

Calling an experienced electrician is the best approach, even for most contractors doing house renovations. The electrician knows how to work safely and successfully with BX cable and metal spiral casing around rubber-insulated wires in which the rubber has deteriorated over time due to air infiltration.

early photographs of the original high-paneled wainscoting and the **oak plate rail,** which had been removed by an earlier owner. To achieve the **authentic Craftsman-style design,** a restoration architect interpreted photographs to re-create the plate rail.

■ ■ The **built-in sideboard** provides the stylistic reference for selecting the **Craftsman-style dining-room table,** its wooden construction as decorative as its simple design is honest. The table, like the sideboard, details the structural peg motif at stress points.

■ ■ **Original oak French doors,** leading from the dining room and living room to respective rear porches, are ingeniously crafted with convex-concave door jambs. Nine doors discovered deep in storage were lovingly restored in a natural wood finish to enhance the dining room's design, light, ventilation, and outdoor

The renovated and enlarged kitchen in the Chester house. The original window above the sink, *left,* provided the core of the renovation plan. The architect adapted the design of Sears-catalog cabinetry for the cabinetry and the scale of the central island, which contains a convection and gas oven. The copper-hooded stove is also a period-style feature, and quite practical above the professional-quality, built-in gas stove. Georgia heart pine from the original floor was matched with new pine to cover the floor area in the expanded kitchen. The stairway to the basement guest room is in the foreground.

A view from the other end of the renovated and enlarged kitchen and breakfast nook in the Chester house. The architect matched the broken pediment trim in the original house to the new addition. Bungalow principles of brightness, simplicity, and efficiency guided the restoration design.

The Brownes' restoration design mixes contemporary technology with period-style design, with the contemporary dishwasher, refrigerator, and stove unconcealed but dominated by the woodenness of the original maple floor, the re-created tin ceiling, and the popular Arts and Crafts gingko-leaf stenciling along the frieze, designed by artist Helen Foster and executed for the owner by River Forest, Illinois, artist Royce Kennedy.

integration with the east-facing porch, where the family enjoys informal dinners on balmy evenings.

■ ■ Repositioning lighting fixtures produces higher and more even light levels through the room while retaining the historic integrity. The original sconces, installed near the sideboard end of the room, diffused limited light across the table, apparently blocked by ceiling beams at the lighted end; shifting sconces to the other end resulted in higher light levels. The hanging lamp is a Stickley adaptation by Rejuvenation.

CHESTER HOUSE, WASHINGTON, D.C.
COLONIAL REVIVAL STYLE

■ ■ **Wooden finishes** in the heart-pine floor and dark-stained walnut trim contrast the natural ivory-painted walls, a simple yet elegant restoration design free of patterned wallpaper or stenciling to focus on the natural woodenness in the neoclassical room.

■ ■ The Moorish-style dining-room table and sideboard complement the neoclassic styling of the room's archi-

ADDING ON: AN ARCHITECT JOINS NEW WITH OLD

"We both love to cook, but we kept getting in each other's way whenever we cooked together, which was about every day," says Ms. Chester. The inadequate counter space, the water damage to areas of the original pine floor, and a desire for a casual eating area and more cooking space compelled the Chesters to add on to their kitchen.

With five years to plan, they were able to outline exactly what they wanted. Fine design and sensitivity to the spirit and scale of the historic bungalow topped the list. As a doctor and lawyer accustomed to deliberate procedures, they approached the kitchen addition with due diligence, interviewing several architects and design-build contractors who had both restored and designed additions to historic houses.

The Chesters immediately excluded the contractors. "We both think that design is very different from building; they are different skills," Ms. Chester explains. "Building is technical; design requires judgment and vision, thinking

about lines, light, space, angles, the aesthetics."

They chose James Pandula of Blackburn Architects, Washington, D.C., largely because he came highly recommended by their neighbor, an architect they respect. The decision was an agonizing one, Ms. Chester remembers, eventually swayed by Pandula's low-key personal style and the sense that he would provide the time and attention to detail and the sensitivity to budget they were looking for. "Jim also had a very nice portfolio," Ms. Chester adds. "He had interesting work and a wide variety of houses."

Even though the work came in well over the initial budget (due to upgrades made during construction), the Chesters are extremely pleased with the results. They also retained Pandula and Blackburn Architects for a subsequent, unexpected job when a large tree fell through the second-floor roof and first-floor bedroom wall. "I think getting an architect was absolutely essen-

tial to doing the best restoration," says Ms. Chester.

The Chester renovation and addition reflect the owners' informal living style, which mixes family and guest functions in the kitchen. The Chesters doubled their kitchen space while fully honoring the character of the original early-twentieth-century Craftsman- and neocolonial-style bungalow, religiously adhering to the Sears-catalog design.

Yet the kitchen is thoroughly modern in its technology and its multi-purpose functions, including food preparation and storage, informal dining, entertaining, relaxing, and even household desk work. The architect's genius lies in re-creating historic window moldings, cabinetry, and scale, while defining distinct areas without closing them off or separating them from the overall space, including a two-workstation area, central island, small breakfast nook, small home office, and built-in storage cabinets.

The Prairie-style radiator covers throughout the Browne house, designed and crafted by carpenter Tony Aducci in the 1990s, look as if they could have been original to this 1916 bungalow. Aducci achieved the woodwork's patina, a finish that usually comes from wood ripening with age, by "fuming" quarter-sawn oak with ammonia, a process in which the tannic acid in the oak reacts with ammonia fumes in a sealed space. The lamps throughout the dining room were created for the owner by Craftsman Footsteps; the natural matte finish on the oak bases was produced by diluting the strength of amber shellac 50 percent with alcohol.

The Montgomerys' restoration kitchen sconce, adapted from a period design of an authentic glasswork lamp, is designed by Michael Adams, New York.

tecture in an **eclectic mix of Arts and Crafts motifs.**

▪▪ The **kitchen renovation** centers around and re-creates the original placement of the sink and the casement windows above, in keeping with the design heritage of bungalow kitchens that recommends **east-facing windows above the sink work space.** The original sink/window location guided the restoration design of new counter areas, a cooking island, built-in cabinets, a dishwasher, stove, and refrigerator.

▪▪ **Built-in kitchen cabinetry** and **storage cabinets** in the adjacent desk area (the original utility porch) and also in the bedroom are patterned after the 1920s Sears-catalog cabinetry design, reinforcing the genuine bungalow spirit in this contemporary renovation.

▪▪ The kitchen's **natural and bright color scheme**

reflects streams of light through groups of windows over the sink and in the breakfast-nook addition: honey-oak, heart-pine flooring (matched from the original hardwood flooring around the sink area only), white Corian countertops, white enamel trim, and muted yellow enamel on cabinets.

BROWNE HOUSE, CHICAGO, ILLINOIS
CRAFTSMAN STYLE

▪▪ The Craftsman-style environment is created by **high-paneled wainscoting, the plate rail, and the box-beam ceiling** design, all added by the owner.

▪▪ **Lamps and lighting fixtures,** Craftsman- and Prairie-style adaptations by Louis G. Glesmann, are essential details in solidifying the room's stylistic provenance.

▪▪ **Authentic antiques mix with new reproductions and inexpensive collectibles** to produce a true Craftsman-style environment, taking good advantage of the lower cost of certain contemporary accessories, such as place settings from T. J. Maxx, lamp bases from Target, generic pottery, and Arts and Crafts-style art from local flea markets.

▪▪ Reinforcing the Craftsman-style ambiance with complementary Prairie-style influences, the **oak radiator covers,** designed and built by carpenter Tony Aducci of Berwyn, Illinois, enhance the room's woodenness and natural patina.

The Montgomery kitchen before restoration.

This precise restoration in the Montgomery kitchen emphasizes the simplicity and healthfulness found throughout the house. The 1920s gas-fired Wedgewood stove, reproduction cabinets and hardware, and suspended Holophane glass lamps complement the authentic white-enamel sink and ivory-enameled cabinetry with pine countertops. The square room responds to Arts and Crafts proponents' fanaticism about efficiency, while the casement windows over the sink fill the room with light and fresh air. This restoration-style kitchen, while a beautiful space, lacks functional counter space and stove/oven equipment that contemporary uses often demand. In fact, the Montgomerys' cook prefers to prepare meals off-site in a 1990s kitchen, while the electric dishwasher, concealed to the left behind a flour-bin cabinet front, improves cleanup.

■■ In the kitchen, **selective Craftsman-style details,** including the pressed-tin ceiling (upgraded from a fluorescent drop ceiling) and the frieze's gingko-leaf stenciling, designed by Helen Foster and executed by Royce Kennedy of River Forest, define the Arts and Crafts context of this contemporary kitchen with 1970s appliances, providing compatible restoration-style references to other rooms of the house.

MONTGOMERY HOUSE,
HOLLYWOOD, CALIFORNIA
MISSION STYLE

■■ Original **Gustav Stickley oak ladder-back chairs** at the table and **Mission-style oak leather-back chairs** (the owner's favorites) lining the edge of the picture window, define the room's plain and direct restoration-style character, completed by the square chestnut dining table and the Stickley oak sideboard in the corner.

■■ **Ceramic pottery** crafted in nature's motifs of flora and fauna provide decorative artisan accents around the room, complemented by wrought-iron candlesticks and the landscape oil over the fireplace mantel.

■■ The unpainted brick fireplace, a rare bungalow element, actually enhances the Mission Revival-style ambiance; it is also a practical heating source in this house's spread-out ground level on chilly days. The ethereal 1920s **California plein-air painting,** commissioned for the house and acquired by the current owners, hangs above the mantel to emphasize the fireplace's prominence in the room.

■■ The **kitchen pantry** offers a near-perfect period-style picture of the **simple, sanitary environment** Arts and Crafts kitchen designers seek, created with an open floor plan unobstructed by furniture for efficient movement, and framed by built-in cabinets that hold reproduction Roycroft day china. The pantry and kitchen

A place setting in the Montgomery dining room follows perfect restoration styling with everyday Roycroft china in one of two early-twentieth-century patterns reproduced by the Roycroft Shops in East Aurora, New York.

The highly ornate Moorish-style sideboard in the Portners' dining room follows the darker-cast influences of some Arts and Crafts interiors, found mostly in dark-wooded Mission Revival-style interiors that mix Mediterranean influences.

cabinetry is designed after an original linen cabinet in the second-floor hallway. The muted ivory enamel paint ensures washability and brightness.

■■ The **1920s kitchen design** appears a time warp in contemporary life, as does the large enamel sink naturally lighted and ventilated with a line of casements above, the restored Wedgwood gas stove, and built-in storage cabinets within easy reach for dry foods. A period-style cabinet front between the stove and sink conceals a contemporary dishwasher.

PORTNER HOUSE,
CHICAGO, ILLINOIS
MOORISH AND TUDOR REVIVAL STYLES

■■ The medieval-style **Moorish Revival sideboard,** an Arts and Crafts accessory style and the most decorative carved piece in the house, provides a focal point for the room, on axis with the room's wide French doors.

■■ The **Jacobean-style carved oak table and uphol-stered chairs,** though originating from two different sets, complement the medieval manner of the Tudor-style oak wall paneling and Moorish-style sideboard.

■■ The blue **Chinese deco rug** dating from the early 1930s is a centerpiece in the vibrant accents of this dark-stained mahogany room, an authentic Arts and Crafts piece that an American patron commissioned a Chinese rug dealer to make and ship to the States.

■■ **Built-in window benches** lining the picture window conceal hot-air radiators and soften the uphol-stered treatment in this formal bungalow dining room.

■■ The polished brass **four-lamp chandelier** and the **original wall sconces** required **rewiring by a profes-sional electrician** with expertise in early-twentieth-century houses, the original cloth wiring having frayed. As is often found in residential restorations, wiring installed after 1950 had been crossed with the original, a real fire hazard only an experienced electrician can adequately address. Most building contractors, in fact, contract out electrical work to licensed electricians.

■■

The Montgomery house second bedroom. This bedroom adjoins a bathroom and a third small bedroom on the other side. Similar to the master bedroom, the restoration style follows Mission Revival influences with natural oak furniture and bright American Indian blankets and rugs. Windows on three sides bring in natural light and look out to the treetops and surrounding landscape.

THE BEDROOM & BATH

THE BUNGALOW BEDROOM IS BRIGHT, CHEERFUL, AND WELL-VENTILATED. THE RESTORATION STYLING, AS THE ORIGINAL DESIGN, IS INTENDED TO PROVIDE a restful and quiet place. In plan, bedrooms tend to be clustered in one separate area of the house, often secluded from the public living-room, dining-room, and kitchen areas. ▪▪ The design of the typical 1910s–1920s bungalow placed the principal two or three bedrooms on the ground floor, adjacent to or adjoining the house's one full bathroom. Second-floor bedrooms and bathrooms are more

common in larger bungalows (Montgomery) and Chicago bungalows designed for a colder climate (Portner), filling out the floor area under the roof structure. Indeed, in most moderate-sized bungalows, the second-floor space was often built as a trunk room or attic under the exposed roof structure; subsequent owners often finish off the area under the gable ridge as a low-ceilinged guest room with beaded oak paneling, the gable-end window providing air and light, as in the Chester house.

Restoration designs of bedrooms and bathrooms, taken together, usually involve two goals: creating additional bedroom space, both on the second floor and the basement level,

and adding at least one full bathroom and usually one half-bathroom to the house.

The original floor plan defines the scope of options available to a bungalow homeowner. The Phelps house, for example, accommodated five second-floor bedrooms and a full bathroom under the broad and spacious gable-roof structure. In the Browne house, the owner adapted the original two bedrooms on the ground level into a guest room and a library, and renovated the second floor with the master bedroom and full bathroom at the highest point under the gable ridge, a low-ceilinged bedroom below the gable slope, and a television sitting room across the length of the gable span. During the restorations of the Chester house, originally built with only two ground-floor bedrooms and standing on a site sloping down toward the rear of the property, the owners built-out the basement level as a guest room/bathroom suite opening out to the backyard through period-style French doors, and on the second floor raised the slope of the hip roof slightly when it was repaired to make room for a second guest room and full bathroom.

The sleeping porch, a trademark feature of early-twentieth-century bungalows, offers another option for expanding bedroom space. In the Portner house, for example, the wicker-furnished sunroom directly adjacent to the dining room functions as a sitting room throughout most of the year and doubles as an extra guest room for weekend guests or large family gatherings. Up in the treetops, the Montgomerys' master bedroom opens to nature via the sleeping porch—an outdoor room now designed as a day office for the owner—and large-paned windows on the south and east facades. The Chester house's restoration joins into one open space the original master bedroom and its sleeping porch, which faces out to the rear of the house, enlarging the overall bedroom area and creating additional space for a built-in closet and for paneled cabinets designed after the Sears-catalog cabinets.

Overall, the restoration-style bedroom is designed to create a quiet and private place, a room with lighter-toned walls and ceilings that create a bright ambiance by reflecting sunlight in the morning and electric light in the evening. As with other rooms in the bungalow, the bedroom design evolves from specific bungalow values, notably a strong interest in creating a fresh and healthful living environment for each individual. Almost a century later, these same values apply to restoration design, just as they do to contemporary bedroom planning:

The Montgomery house master bedroom before restoration.

The Montgomery house master bedroom and sleeping porch. The bedroom restoration style follows Mission Revival influences with colorful American Indian textiles set against the golden hue of naturally stained oak furniture and floors. The sleeping porch, restored as an informal office with desk and chair, was added to the master bedroom soon after construction of the original house was completed in 1910–11.

The Chester house master bedroom. The owners' most recent restoration combined the original bedroom and sleeping porch into one large space, opening at the back of the house. The restoration style emphasizes overall simplicity in furnishings, heightening the impact of the natural light. The owners' architect and contractor, who completed the first restoration, matched the window and doorway trim on the original house, pulled up floor-to-floor carpeting, refinished white and fir pine floors with light sanding and natural stain, and added a stronger beam between the original room and porch to reinforce support for the upstairs area. Pale yellow and white Benjamin Moore paint on walls and trim, respectively, enhance the room's brightness.

IMPROVING VENTILATION ON THE SECOND FLOOR

The Chesters' second-floor restoration became an emergency job when an old oak tree fell through the hip roof during a rain and wind storm on April 1, 1997. "We had no more than a month to plan," says Ms. Chester, "so we worked with Jim [James Pandula of Blackburn Architects] and his computerized simulation of the roofline to design the expansion of the second-floor area." (Pandula also designed and oversaw the kitchen addition and restoration.)

The Chesters raised the back roof slope slightly, creating a modified gable from a low-pitched hip roof, and also added a shed-roof dormer to the rear. Both changes are evident from the rear yet not detectable to public view from the front of the house. The bungalow's original Craftsman-style exterior design was a key consideration, and remains preserved.

The emergency restoration provided an opportunity to improve insulation and air circulation. Because insulation between rafters must have year-round ventilation to allow moisture to escape, the overhanging roof eaves provide a good place to conceal ventilators. The architect installed soffit vents in the wide eave areas to allow the intake of fresh outside air.

In addition, another vent was placed on top of the rear roof to permit warm moist air to escape. The ventilator is flush with the roof to prevent rain and snow seepage, and the placement on the rear slope made it invisible from the front of the house.

■■ Quiet: The bedroom is separated from public living areas by a private hall (Phelps house) or located in a distinct and secluded area of the house, often on the second floor under the roof structure (Montgomery and Portner houses) or behind solid wood-paneled doors (Browne and Chester houses).

■■ Light: Sited to receive morning sun and adequate natural light throughout the day, the bedroom is designed with an abundant window area through groups of casements, or French doors/windows when facing a private patio at the rear. Walls covered with a light-toned or muted paint or paper, particularly white or ivory enamel, enhance brightness and illumination.

■■ Freshness: The bedroom is a moderately spacious room with operable windows (casements, ideally) designed for fresh-air ventilation and cross-circulation and, ideally, closets vented with fresh-air shafts to the roof.

■■ Cleanliness: A minimalist decor of light and washable fabrics and simply crafted furniture creates a fresh and sanitary environment; furnishings are chosen for their function in the room rather than their ornamental appeal, including bed, bedstand, a low dresser with wall mirror, and perhaps a sitting chair and small desk.

■■ Healthfulness: Designed in proximity to the bathroom—typically adjoining it—the bedroom emphasizes the individual's well-being in a fresh, light, airy, and quiet environment.

Restoration designs for bungalow bedrooms follow one of two approaches: one, a plain, sparse, almost ascetic styling, with walls and ceilings painted white or ivory enamel, and furniture limited to only functional pieces, such as the Chester and Montgomery houses; or two, a decorative styling in warm and deep colors creating a dense and comfortable ambiance through wallpaper and stenciling, fabrics and Arts and Crafts deco, and acces-

The Portner house ground-floor bathroom. The original porcelain floor, cast-iron enamel toilet and sink, and ceramic tiles have been well maintained over the years and carefully cleaned with nontoxic chemical cleansers. The window, an indispensable feature in bungalow bathrooms (as in bedrooms) is essential for ventilation and light.

sory as well as functional furnishings, such as the Browne and Phelps houses.

THE BATH

The bungalow bathroom, finished in white or ivory porcelain with nickel-plate fixtures, is designed in the same spirit of cleanliness, freshness, and brightness that permeates the kitchen. Walls of white rectangular ceramic tile (Portner house) and enameled, creamy white-painted, pearled woodwork (Chester house) are designed for easy cleaning. The high-paneled or -tiled wainscot wall, at three-quarters or half height, is bordered at the top by a narrow cornice or tiles laid horizontally. (Colored ceramic tiles arrived in the

The Montgomery house ground-floor bathroom. For this completely fabricated room, the architect covered walls and ceiling with naturally stained oak-beaded paneling and installed an antique pull-chain toilet, found by the project team's antiquing scout, to achieve an authentic period-style restoration.

American bathroom in the 1920s, often as an accent band.)

Carried over from the Victorian era when the mechanized bathroom emerged, the bungalow bathroom is characterized by cast-iron fixtures finished in porcelain, including the toilet, hot and cold running water, the claw-foot bathtub, the standing shower, and the embedded wall medicine cabinet. Quite often, built-in linen and toiletry cabinets frame the bathroom or the adjacent bathroom-bedroom hallway, such as in the Montgomery house. Craftsmanship in the bathroom respects a level of restraint, focusing on the plainly milled oak- or mahogany-trimmed medicine cabinet and towel racks, the built-in cabinetry, and the porcelain-tile floor of small hexagonal tiles set in creamy white or white and black. One or two small, operable windows, preferably casements, welcome in light and fresh air.

Adapting a period-style bathroom to contemporary use entails very little in the way of structural and design alterations. The greater part of the adaptation is social, revolving around the owner's personal expectations about contemporary bathroom design. A full period bathroom, as in the Montgomery house, with claw-foot tub and pedestal sink, lacks such features as expansive counter space for toiletries, double sinks, and strong water pressure to rapidly fill a deep claw-foot tub. Period-style toilets are narrower and higher than contemporary toilets; water-tap fixtures divide hot-and-cold water faucets, rather than unifying the tap with temperature-controlled water.

In the Chester restoration, the owner chose to remove the original master bathroom, which had deteriorated and been substantially altered over time, and re-create a period-style bathroom with reproduction fixtures. Still, the architect remained sensitive to the room's refined scale in the hexagonal porcelain floor tiles, tap fixtures, and even the enameled wood wainscoting patterned after the Sears catalog.

RESTORATION-STYLE BEDROOMS AND BATHROOMS

■ ■

BROWNE HOUSE, CHICAGO, ILLINOIS
CRAFTSMAN STYLE

■ ■ Natural tones of **greens and browns** and **paper and fabric patterns** adapted from original designs create the ambiance of this guest room; Bradbury & Bradbury "Fir Tree" border paper accents the muted moss green paint, the Morris reproduction Willow Leaf patterned bedspread, the circa-1900 Eastlake-style bed frame, and the Mission-style baby crib, ice-box dressing table, desk, and chair.

■ ■ The room's **modest size, casement windows,** and **authentic Arts and Crafts furnishings** exemplify bungalow values of freshness, cleanliness, and healthfulness.

■ ■ Located adjacent to the large living room and main doorway entrance, the bedroom's **quiet ambiance** may be compromised by proximity to public areas, yet window coverings, floor rugs, and a ceiling fan provide noise buffers.

■ ■ The **restored original bathroom** showcases the pedestal sink, the embedded oak-trimmed medicine cabinet, the enamel toilet, the small hexagonal porcelain tiles, and the ceramic tiles lining the shower wall with a period-style glass-brick window overhead.

■ ■ Using a personally touching **decorative motif** to strengthen the bathroom styling, Jane Browne show-

The Browne house ground-floor bathroom, also known as the "Theodore Roosevelt Memorial" bathroom for the memorabilia lining the walls and for the provenance of the original fixtures, is from the same period in which Roosevelt occupied the White House. The restoration focused on cleaning the authentic porcelain floor and the enamel toilet and sink with nontoxic chemicals, refinishing the oak-framed medicine cabinet with natural stain, and painting the walls deep moss green to match the "Iris" pattern frieze paper, Bradbury & Bradbury.

cased a treasured collection of Theodore Roosevelt etchings, lithographs, portraits, and memorabilia on walls and shelves.

CHESTER HOUSE, WASHINGTON, D. C.
COLONIAL REVIVAL STYLE

■ ■ Combining the master bedroom and the outdoor sleeping porch into one space, the owners chose a **plain and ascetic design** to emphasize **bungalow values of light and freshness,** using muted yellow tones against white wood trim and cotton fabrics; the restoration contractor adapted the plain wood-trim design from the bungalow's original trim.

■ ■ The restored **Douglas pine floor** in the master bedroom, previously lined with wall-to-wall 1970s carpet-

The Chester house ground-floor half-bathroom. The owners added this bathroom to the rear of the expanded kitchen area and relocated an original cast-iron enamel sink and radiator from a previously removed bathroom to this one. The contractor, who has worked with the owners on this and subsequent restoration projects, designed the mirror frame to match the original woodwork in this Sears bungalow.

The Chester house ground-floor master bathroom. The high-paneled beaded wainscoting, painted an authentic white enamel, follows period-style design, as do the porcelain floor with small, white-and-black tiles, the wood trim adapted from original Sears plans, and the original radiator.

ing, is unified with the sleeping porch's higher-grade **white-pine floor** to create a spacious room opening to the private backyard.

■ ■ **Storage** is added by building a wall closet, which backs into the original utility porch space, and tall wooden cabinets designed after original Sears-catalog cabinets.

■ ■ The original **second-floor trunk room** under the large front-facing gable end, lighted by the gable casement window, is **finished as a low-ceilinged guest room** with rustic, honey-toned, beaded-oak paneling.

■ ■ The **rebuilt master bathroom** succeeds as a period-style room with the refined modest scale, the reproduction fixtures and original artifacts, including the high-beaded wainscoting painted enamel white, the hexagonal porcelain-tile floor, the Sears wood trim around the window and doors, and the original hot-air radiator.

MONTGOMERY HOUSE
HOLLYWOOD, CALIFORNIA
MISSION REVIVAL STYLE

■ ■ The **sparsely furnished Mission-style bedrooms** are highlighted with the true colors of American Indian rugs and blankets, creating a light and fresh environment for rest and repose. The master bedroom features an original Gustav Stickley bed and William Morris chair with the original leather upholstery.

■ ■ The **sleeping porch,** added soon after the original house was built and furnished with a Mission-style desk and chair, is designed as a sitting room and day office, a furnished tree house for writing, telephoning, and reading.

■ ■ In the spirit of healthful and efficient design, each of the **three upstairs bedrooms,** which occupy the area under the splaying gable roof, **adjoins a full bathroom,** the two small bedrooms sharing one and the master bedroom adjoining a large bathroom also accessible from the stairhall.

The Phelps house bedroom, ground floor. The original bedrooms, located at the front of the house to receive morning light, adjoin a bathroom on each side. The restoration style is dominated by Bradbury & Bradbury papers on the walls, frieze, and ceiling, adapted from original circa-1880 Walter Crain papers. The painter, who has worked with the owners throughout the house's restoration, custom-mixed the paint for doors and window and doorway trim to match the paper.

■ ■ The **restoration bathroom design** appears as it might have in 1910, with creamy ivory-enamel walls and wood trim, pedestal sinks, a standing shower and a claw-foot tub, medicine cabinets with small attached shelves for toiletries, and porcelain-tiled floors. White, plain, sanitary spaces have been restored in every detail.

■ ■ The **first-floor half-bathroom** follows the **rustic styling** of the main rooms, finished in a honey-toned, beaded-oak paneling with period hardware, notably the pull-chain flush toilet and nickel-plated fixtures.

PHELPS HOUSE, PASADENA, CALIFORNIA
CRAFTSMAN STYLE

■ ■ The **decorative value of Arts and Crafts wall and ceiling papers** is evident in this guest room, originally one of two ground-floor bedrooms. Nature's deeper tones of ochre, earth brown, and terra-cotta enrich three Bradbury & Bradbury papers. Dark-stained wood fur-

The Chester house master bedroom. These closets were designed by the owners' contractor to match period-style Sears-catalog closets.

nishings and dim lighting create a quiet and tranquil setting.

■ ■ **Freshness** is ensured in the two front bedrooms, with fresh air and natural light circulating front to back from these casement windows to operable leaded-glass windows in the hallway, and beyond to the living room.

■ ■ The original front bedrooms and bathroom enjoy **complete privacy** from the central living area, separated from the living room and kitchen by a short hall and enclosed behind slatted window coverings and solid wood-paneled doors.

■ ■ Emphasizing practical planning, the bedroom design includes **spacious walk-in closets;** this sympathetic restoration design blends the rich mocha color of the period-style wall and ceiling papers with the paint of the wood-paneled closet doors.

The Montgomery house linen cabinet, second floor. This naturally finished, oak-paneled linen cabinet, the only original cabinet left in the house when the owner bought it, provided the architect's reference for restoring all period-style cabinetry in the house, including the kitchen, the library, and the study.

The Chester house front porch. Measuring an expansive 26 feet long by 10 feet deep on this modestly scaled house, the porch was restored to heighten the presence of this traditional home element. The owners scraped off flaking paint, primed the frame wood with a sealant, and repainted in natural brown, gray, and green tones that heighten the Craftsman styling of the columns and piers, the deep eaves and brackets, and the timber-frame pattern in the gable end.

CHAPTER SEVEN

THE PORCH & SUNROOM

Porches and sunrooms define the bungalow's communal character and domestic face. The porch epitomizes the bungalow's integration of house and land, architecture and landscape, structure and nature: it reaches from interior living spaces to the outdoors and, conversely, from the broader landscape and community into the narrower domain of the familial household. Because the porch can accommodate many activities—eating, sleeping, reading, lounging, entertaining, and working—it offers the homeowner wonderful flexibility in living arrangements.

Four general types of porches are common to bungalows around the country: front porch, back porch, sunroom, and sleeping porch.

Front Porch

The bungalow's outdoor living room reflects early-twentieth-century habits of front-porch sitting and socializing with one's neighbors. Manifest architecturally, these open shelters define the character of the bungalow's face, distinguished by low-slung roofs, wide eaves, and, often, columns shaped in artistic forms, as in the Chester house with its sloped piers and grouped columns. Bungalows with prominent front porches, such as the Chester and Montgomery houses, are designed deep for sitting and lounging, and wide to take in multiple activities at once, often extending the entire front of the house. Not unusual, the Chester porch measures 26 feet long by 10 feet deep, and the Montgomery porch is 42 feet long and 13 feet deep, in proportion with the larger bungalow.

The front porch may be integrated within the main roof, blending stylistically in materials and colors with the bungalow structure, as in the Montgomery house, clad as it is in natural cedar-shingle siding and a floor and solid wall of matching dark brown paint. During the restoration, the architect Martin Eli Weil restored the front-facing porch wall by replacing rotted cedar shingles on the front with well-aged shingles from the rear of the house (replacing those with new cedar shingles) and by painting the porch wall and window trim with re-created versions of the original dark brown and deep forest green colors, respectively. The Adirondack-style chairs, painted deep forest green, remain on the porch year-round, covered as they are by the overhanging eaves.

The front porch may alternatively appear as an extension of the main block, as in the Chester house, covered by a roof structure separate from the principal roofline and presenting a contrasting element in the architectural form and the color scheme. During the restoration, for example, the owners developed a natural color scheme of muted beige-brown and deep green on the dominant Craftsman-style details of bracketed eaves, front-facing gable, and pebble-stuccoed facade to heighten the effect of the porch's broad outlines and decorative value. They complemented this with a creamy ivory on the timber-frame gable end to dramatize the decorative detail, and with a light stone gray on the porch interior to diminish the visual impact of the large floor area.

BACK PORCH

The bungalow back porch tends not to be as commodious as the front porch, with larger porches appearing in southern California, the Southwest, and the South, where several months of balmy weather lead to backyard living and an outdoor lifestyle. The Phelps California bungalow is typical of many California bungalows, designed with large porches (this one, 25 feet long by 6 feet deep) facing the backyard and terrace and extending out from the south-facing living room. The Phelpses restored the rear porch by reinstalling the original Craftsman-style oak French doors that open between the

The Phelps house rear solarium porch, *left,* and rear dining-room porch, *right.* Cathy Phelps, a restoration designer, re-created the original screened porch opening off the living room by reinstalling the Craftsman-style oak French doors between house and porch, doors the previous owner had removed and stored, and replacing/staining the shingles to match the house. The owners plan to complete the dining-room porch restoration by re-creating the original, solid, wood-paneled half-wall; the Phelpses have reinstalled the original French doors leading out from the dining room as part of this room's restoration, and stained and painted shingles and trim, respectively, to integrate the porch with the overall house.

The Chester house rear porch, deck, and patio. As part of the kitchen renovation and expansion, the rear of the house was reconstructed with a new upper-level porch, deck and stairs, and patio, creating an outdoor living and cooking area to integrate the original bungalow with the site and extend the activities of the house outward to the rear yard. Blackburn Architects, which designed the restoration, matched exterior siding with the siding on the original house and created a new gable end to match the front-porch gable with the timber-frame pattern. The porch railings, columns, and the pergola reflect the front porch's scale and design.

The Montgomery house enclosed rear porch-like room. Monty Montgomery's rear study leads out to a private fieldstone patio, enclosed as an indoor-outdoor room with screens replacing windows in this southern California climate. Restoration architect Martin Eli Weil and contractor Tim Kelly sanded and refinished the reddish-toned Douglas fir wood floor in a transparent glazing, then stripped paint and stained the natural mahogany on the walls. The owners' Adirondack- and Mission-style furnishings complete the rustic environment.

living room and porch, and installing specially designed darker screens on all sides, sympathetic with the dark forest-green tone of the bungalow's shingles. Adjacent to the living-room porch is the east-facing porch, opening out through the dining room and Craftsman-style French doors. Previous owners had altered the bungalow character of this porch by installing colonial-style railings all around: restoration-style bungalows tend not to have open-post railings on the rear porch, and neocolonial railings are incompatible with a Craftsman-style bunga-

low. Time and finances permitting, the Phelpses plan to restore the porch to its original design, bordered by a solid frame half-wall (similar to the Montgomery house) and painted dark charcoal gray or dark forest green.

Back porches designed for storage rather than lounging, originally called utility porches, follow a functional design appropriate to a smaller enclosed space. The Chester and Portner houses were originally built with utility porches at the back, measuring approximately 12 feet long and 4 feet deep, both of

The Montgomery house front porch. Extending across the house's main block, the porch measures 42 feet long by 13 feet deep, sheltered by the roof's deep overhanging eaves. During restoration, all the original thirteen-foot hand-cut cedar shingles in good condition on exterior surfaces replaced rotted shingles on the front facade, thus ensuring an authentic presentation on the public face. New three-foot machine-sawn shingles replaced rotted shingles on side and rear facades. The floor is repainted the original dark brown color, matching the natural cedar-shingle finish; the deep forest green window trim recreates the original trim paint color; and the reproduction Adirondack-style deck chairs reflect the Arts and Crafts style.

The Portner house rear solarium. Typical of many bungalows, this windowed and screened sunroom opens off the formal dining room and is used as an informal eating and sitting room as well as an extra guest room. The birch window trim, quite fortunately, had never been painted; the owners refurbished the wood with a light transparent stain. This sun-bleached space is furnished with period-style, antique wicker chairs and a settee, and an authentic oak Stickley armchair.

A view from the Browne sunroom into the living-room area. Natural light from the sunroom windows highlights the earthy colors and textures the Brownes chose for this room, including the muted mocha brown wall paint (Benjamin Moore), the natural oak and wicker furniture, and the stripped and unpainted raw-brick fireplace.

The Browne house front sunroom, integrated with the living-room area. Before the current owners' purchase, the original front sunroom and living room were opened into one space, with the interconnecting French doors removed. The Brownes have maximized the effect of light and the room's openness by stripping windows and wood trim of paint to expose the natural oak and leaving windows free of drapes and shades.

which have been removed. The Chesters incorporated the utility porch, originally used for cold-food storage, into the kitchen expansion; the Portners' porch was removed by previous owners who built an incompatible cedar rear deck that the Portners intend to replace with a period-style porch.

SUNROOM

In the spirit of healthfulness and indoor-outdoor integration, the sunroom offers the flexibility of serving different functions, including an informal living or dining room, a guest room, and an enclosed porch. The sunroom is built as an integrated room within the body of the main house or as a projecting element, exposed on three sides and framed by windows and/or screens all around. The sunrooms of the Portner and Montgomery houses extend from the dining rooms, measuring approximately 14 by 13 feet and serving as informal eating areas or even guest rooms.

The Portner sunroom is styled in a manner consistent with the interior's eclectic Arts and Crafts styling, furnished with white-enamel wicker and colorful floral cushions. Unpainted and naturally stained Douglas fir trim around curtainless windows complements the bright surface of plain, ivory-painted plaster walls. The Montgomery sunroom, similarly, is framed by the natural cedar-shingle walls of the exterior and furnished with rustic Adirondack-style chairs and table. During the day, the brilliantly lit, private sunroom takes in the breeze of abutting trees, looking out over the property's rocky landscape. By night, the city of Los Angeles spreads out in a colorful panorama of lights to the south.

The Montgomery house enclosed dining-room porch. Opening off the dining room, this screened-in porch is used for informal dining and sitting. Added soon after the original house was completed, the porch is covered with cedar-shingle walls that the owner cleaned and stained with natural finish. The floor is painted a dark brown and the trim a deep forest green to match the original design as well as the front porch, which this leads out to. Adirondack-style furniture reinforces the outdoor Arts and Crafts style.

The Montgomery house Adirondack-style chair, part of an early-twentieth-century set chosen by Roger L. Conant Williams, the owners' Arts and Crafts curator and designer.

SLEEPING PORCH

The sleeping porch of the night, extending out from the main bedroom, is transformed into an outdoor sitting room during the day. Sleeping porches are most often found in period bungalows located in the Southwest and in southeastern states such as Virginia, North Carolina, Georgia, and Florida.

The Montgomerys' sleeping porch opens to a southern exposure off the master bedroom through uncurtained French doors, sitting as a tree house amid the treetops. Measuring 15 feet long by 9 feet deep, the original sleeping porch has been restored as an informal day office for the owner, sparsely furnished with a Mission Revival-style oak desk and chair, and accessorized with the contemporary technology of telephone and fax machine, as well as an old Arts and Crafts magazine stand turned bookshelf.

The original Chester sleeping porch in Washington, D.C., has now been combined with the original master bedroom into one enlarged, unified room, with the bed placed so as to receive the eastern morning sun.

The Montgomery house master-bedroom sleeping porch. Measuring 15 feet long by 9 feet deep, the original sleeping porch, known as an "outdoor bedroom," has been restored as an informal office with Mission Revival-style oak desk and chair. Shingle wall surfaces have been cleaned and stained, and the floor is repainted in the original dark brown tone; screens here and throughout the house are re-created from the original design, using a darker, period-style screen web, not the lighter aluminum screen of contemporary houses.

The Phelps house living room. The light golden ochre grass-cloth wall covering and the natural fumed-oak trim meld with the unpainted brick of the fireplace inglenook. All surfaces have remained unpainted since construction in 1908; the Phelpses cleaned, lightly sanded, and naturally stained the oak window, wall, and ceiling trim.

NATURE'S COLORS, CRAFTS, & MATERIALS

THE ARTISTIC PRESENTATION AND THE CRAFTSMANSHIP OF NATURE'S MATE-RIALS AND NATURE'S COLORS ARE KEYS TO THE ENDURING VALUE AND restoration design of the bungalow, perhaps second only to its architectural appeal. The ingenious furniture designer Gustav Stickley may be largely credited with the sustained interest in the architectural forms and furnishings derived from nature and natural materials. In restoration design, nature's beauty can be found in the tone, texture, composition, and functional purpose of nature-made materials,

materials worthy of methodical restoration and maintenance in a vintage bungalow. The continuity of authentic Arts and Crafts elements throughout the house will heighten the effect and the success of a bungalow restoration. The goal is to create exterior and interior restoration styles that harmonize in color, finish, and stylistic manner with the architecture. The wonderful interplay between wood, stone, metal, wool, silk, burlap, cotton, and ceramic, and the simple artistry of a table, chair, and sideboard against the complex artistry of art-glass windows, carved rafter ends, and veg-etable-dyed Indian rugs creates the animus of an authentic bungalow residence.

NATURE'S MATERIALS

Indigenous regional materials blend best with the tones and textures of the immediate environment, as seen in the cedar shingles of the Montgomery and Phelps houses. Restoring these materials to their natural state, such as the golden brown brick of the Portner house and the shingles of the Montgomery house in southern California, thus enhances both these elements and the complementary features in the composition, such as brick-enhancing limestone and a band of stained-glass windows. In this way, the house regains an essential familiarity with its setting, especially when the surrounding property is left in its natural state,

The restored second-floor trunk room in the Chester house, under the front gable area, is now a charming, oak-paneled guest room, naturally lighted by the gable's casement window.

as in the arid and rocky landscape of the Montgomerys' Hollywood hills house.

Likewise, restoring and maintaining the natural wood and stone of the architecture (through cleaning, replacement, and restaining) establishes an important link between the building and the region in which it stands: cedar and fieldstone in the West, adobe in the Southwest, stucco and limestone in the Mid-Atlantic, sandstone in the Midwest, and pine in the South. For example, the Montgomery house's restoration architect restored the split fieldstone with its irregular markings and colors to enhance the tone of the restored woodwork and strengthen the rugged effect of the

Mission Revival-style design and its connection with the southern California land. To do so, the architect made a necessary like-kind replacement of indigenous stone by shipping in a truckload of young fieldstone from a riverbed in the Southwest to supplement the original granite on-site.

Throughout the country, the use of regional materials has had a powerful influence on the styling and design of vernacular domestic architecture. Unarguably, the hundreds of thousands of mail-order bungalows built around the country have diminished a certain amount of regionalism. Yet in contemporary restoration design, the key is to restore wood, stone, metal, and ceramic materials to a natural condition or natural color, remaining sympathetic to the design heritage as well as to contemporary needs and living standards.

NATURE'S COLORS AND SOURCES

Restoration-style colors derive from nature's resources. Warm and muted hues of earth, fire, water, and sun create the authentic bungalow spirit, complementing deeper tones of wood and stone. Nature's crafts, as well, focus on the life of the soil in the prominent use of pinecones, gingko leaves, and roses in etchings, fabrics, pottery, embroidery, wallpaper, and picture frames.

"Natural" and "simple" bungalow scenes actually require complex thought and often several interviews of different artisans and contractors: it takes deliberate planning to adorn plaster walls with dusky olive-yellow burlap or a lighter golden tone; to preserve a rubblestone or raw brick fireplace; to achieve a

Pottery in the Montgomery house, shaped by the foliage of nature.

patina finish on natural timber beams and a wet mossy green or muted ochre on ceiling panels. (Ceiling surfaces require a lighter tone than walls and floors to reflect light and bring out the deeper values of the woodwork.)

Arts and Crafts restoration design diffuses the sharp contrasts between positive and negative tones and colors, as well as shapes and textures. Warmth, comfort, and serenity derive from muted colors; strong colors tend to be jarring. In the same way, an exterior foundation of natural stone and brown cedar shakes blends

WORKING WITH NATURE'S ARTISTS

Jane Browne epitomizes the wanna-be artist and architect that exists in every historic homeowner to some degree. "I am an addict for Craftsman design," she says, "and I love to create scenes and comfortable places to sit in my house."

While Browne's creative energies are essential to the artistry of the restoration, the quality of her period-style bungalow also stems from the great pleasure she takes in systematically prowling antique markets for Craftsman and Mission Revival pieces, and from her friendships with Arts and Crafts artisans who create lamps, wall hangings, embroidered fabrics, stenciling, pottery, Prairie-style radiator covers and railings, as well as those who can strip coats of paint from an original oak trim and restore it to its natural tawny finish. Such professional friendships with designer Paul Duchscherer, lamp makers Paul Glesmann and Steward Surfer, and contractor and painter Tony Aducci stand her in good stead as she renovates; they become sympathetic to her house's restoration style and to her family's personal style.

The color scheme of the Chester house references the muted tones found in nature, including the golden beige paint of the porch stucco, the deep forest green of trim and gable eaves and brackets, and the creamy ivory of the clapboard siding and timber-framing in the gable ends. The muted gray of the porch floor and the roof shingles provides a neutral background against the brown and green tones.

The Phelpses carefully devised the exterior color scheme to reflect architect Roehrig's original design, with the deep forest green shingle stain on walls (the original roof color) and the deep brown asphalt roof (the original shingle wall stain), while choosing a livelier pumpkin orange trim rather than the dark burnt orange of the period.

RESTORING NATURE IN THE EXTERIOR

Exterior restorations focus on cleaning, refinishing, and rebuilding the tone, texture, and shape of natural materials:

- ■ ■ *Foundation: rubblestone, fieldstone, granite, brick*

- ■ ■ *Walls: shingle, stucco, brick, clapboard*

- ■ ■ *Roof: asphalt, shakes, tar paper*

- ■ ■ *Chimney: rubblestone, fieldstone, granite, brick*

- ■ ■ *Gable ends: frame, half-timber, stucco*

- ■ ■ *Bracketed eaves: wood*

Restoration architect Martin Eli Weil and contractor Tim Kelly restored the Montgomery house's natural cedar shingles by relocating all original thirteen-foot handcut shingles to the front and replacing side and rear facades with contemporary, three-foot machine-cut shingles. California Roof Savers pressure-washed, bleached, and water-blasted the shingles, then they were left to age naturally. The architect matched the window-trim paint to the original dark forest green.

The Prairie-style stairway screen and columns in the Browne house replace a solid wall that effectively compartmentalized this small hallway into divided, discrete spaces. The screen, designed by Arts and Crafts designer Paul Duchscherer, San Francisco, integrates restoration style with a personal desire for openness and natural light, which streams down the stairwell from the second-floor skylight.

with an entrance walk of cut fieldstones, an easy transition of tones found in the Montgomery bungalow. The dark green-stained shingles of the Phelps house blend with the green grass, and the deep charcoal eaves and dark brown asphalt roof surfaces complement the horizon's tree limbs. Even the Phelpses' brilliant sienna orange trim, more dramatic than the original burnt orange, absorbs the bright sun against the deep green, bringing a bright accent to this Craftsman-style design.

These bungalow restorations introduce color into rooms and exterior features in a variety of sources, including rugs, pottery, art-glass lamps, windows, fabrics, textiles, paint, wallpaper and wall cloth, stenciling, embroidery, and eaves brackets and trim. For each bungalow, the styling of a room and one or more architectural elements guide the choice of color families and the strength of tonal values to be applied.

■ ■

The simple beauty of natural oak sideboards with brass hardware emphasizes the craftsmanship and artistry of functional design in the Craftsman and Mission styles. The repetition of such decorative details as the "X" motif provides continuity from room to room.

The creamy ivory enamel paint on walls and cabinets throughout the Montgomery house, including the kitchen, pantry, library, and second-floor bathrooms and bedrooms, emphasizes the natural freshness, brightness, and cleanliness indigenous to bungalow design.

Even in this small period-style bathroom, with original surfaces covered in ivory porcelain and tile, the dominance of the deep green walls creates a design scheme of nature's colors.

The Browne dining-room color scheme stems from the forest, with the deep moss green paint on walls, the fumed quartersawn oak trim, the gingko-leaf table scarf and linens, and appropriately patterned pottery and china.

The folding screen with tanned leather panels was designed and built by Paul Kramer, who tanned the leather and fumed the quartersawn white oak. In the Browne living room, the 68"-high by 66"-wide screen crafted with Arts and Crafts joinery and hardware provides a moveable backdrop for a sitting nook as well as a subtle roof divider.

The bold brass door hardware on the massive oak front door of the Phelps house is a classic feature of California design in the Arts and Crafts genre, whether Craftsman, Mission, Swiss Chalet, or California bungalow style.

The original hanging lantern above the front door of the Montgomery house is a classic California Mission-style design of brass and gold art glass.

This exterior lantern sits atop an entrance column at the base of the fieldstone steps that rise to the front entrance of the Montgomery house. Adapted from a period Mission-style design by Michael Adams, New York, the lantern is made of brass with verdigris patina finish and gold bubble glass.

This mounted Stamford Lantern in solid brass features gold-white art glass and a verdigris patina finish. The popular Stamford design, 1910, features the crossbow pattern, this one with the angular emphasis of California Mission architecture. By Michael Adams, New York, for the Montgomery house.

The leaded-art-glass windows in the Portner house entrance hall and living room showcase the artistic beauty in Arts and Crafts architectural design, integrating nature's most brilliant tones and exploiting rays of sunshine beaming through to light up the indoor rooms.

To refinish the mahogany window and doorway trim in the Chester house, the contractor stripped off the 1918 shellac, then cleaned and re-shellacked the wood. Identical finish replaced the original finish, as appropriate. The excellent condition of the Georgian heart-pine floor throughout the house is due to only three sandings in over eighty years (pine, a softer wood, should be rarely and carefully sanded) and natural, low-luster varnish. For safekeeping, the Chesters have a supply of newly milled heart pine (from North Carolina), used during the kitchen renovation.

The ground-floor bedroom in the Browne house calls on nature's themes in the muted forest green wall paint and the Fir Tree-pattern border paper by Bradbury & Bradbury, as well as the natural-stained oak furniture and the William Morris-reproduction, Willow Leaf-pattern bedspread.

NATURE'S COLORS AND FINISHES: THE FIVE BUNGALOWS

PHELPS HOUSE
EXTERIOR

Siding	Cedar shingle; dark green stain
Foundation	Brick / unpainted
Window trim	Pumpkin orange
Roof	Asphalt shingles; dark brown
Eaves	Cedar; dark charcoal stain

INTERIOR

Living room

Walls	Light golden ochre grass cloth
Floor / trim	Oak / natural stain
Upholstery	Cotton duck fabric / undyed

Dining room

Walls	Light golden ochre grass cloth
Wood trim	Oak / natural stain
Floor	Oak / tongue-in-groove oak
Ceiling	Oak ceiling beam; deep sand-gray paint

Guest room

Walls	Bradbury & Bradbury paper, Walter Crain design
Frieze	Bradbury & Bradbury paper, Walter Crain design
Wood trim	Oak / muted brown paint

BROWNE HOUSE
INTERIOR

Living room

Walls	Muted mocha brown paint, Benjamin Moore
Frieze	Historic Homes Book No. 4 paper
Wood trim	Oak / natural stain
Floor	Oak / natural stain

Dining room

Walls	Oak-paneled wainscoting with moss green paint
Frieze	Muted beige paint / Roycroft Collection-Sherwin Williams
Ceiling	Oak box beam / light ivory paint
Wood trim	Oak / natural stain
Floor	Oak / natural stain

Kitchen

Walls	Plaster / light golden ochre paint
Frieze	Gingko-leaf stencil, pattern by Helen Foster
Ceiling	Pressed tin / creamy ivory enamel paint
Floor	Maple / natural stain

Bedroom

Walls	Muted forest green
Frieze	Bradbury & Bradbury paper, "Fir Tree" pattern
Wood trim	Oak / natural stain
Floor	Oak / natural stain

Bathroom

Walls	Ceramic tile, rectangular
Frieze	Bradbury & Bradbury paper, "Iris" pattern
Floor	Porcelain tile / white
Fixtures	Enameled cast-iron

Library

Walls	Sienna red paint, Roycroft Collection-Sherwin Williams
Frieze	Bradbury & Bradbury paper, "Thornberry" pattern

MONTGOMERY HOUSE
EXTERIOR

Siding	Cedar-shake shingles; 13' original, 3' replacement / natural stain
Window trim	Cedar / deep forest green paint
Roof	Rolled tar paper
Eaves	Cedar / natural stain

INTERIOR

Living room

Walls	Plaster / golden ochre burlap
Floor	Oak / natural stain
Upholstery	Tanned leather
Chairs	Oak / natural stain
Ceiling	Mahogany paneling and beams / unwaxed natural stain
Bookcases	Mahogany / unwaxed natural stain

Dining room

Walls	Mahogany wainscot paneling / unwaxed natural stain
	Plaster / golden ochre burlap
Floor	Oak / natural stain
Trim	Mahogany / unwaxed natural stain
Ceiling	Mahogany paneling / unwaxed natural stain
Fireplace	Brick / unpainted

Kitchen

Walls	Plaster / ivory enamel paint
Floor	Pine / natural stain
Cabinets	Pine / ivory enamel paint
Counters	Pine / natural

Study

Walls	Fir paneling / natural transparent glaze
Ceiling	Plaster / ivory flat paint
Floor	Douglas fir / mahogany stain
Trim	Fir / natural glaze

Porch

Walls	Cedar shingle / natural
Floor	Cedar / dark brown paint (match natural shingles)
Trim	Cedar / deep forest green paint

Bedroom

Walls	Pine / ivory enamel paint
Ceiling	Pine / ivory enamel paint
Floor	Oak / natural stain

Bathroom

Walls	Ivory enamel paint
Floor	Porcelain hexagonal tiles
Fixtures	Cast-iron enamel

PORTNER HOUSE
EXTERIOR

Siding	Brick / unpainted
Trim	Limestone / unpainted
Roof	Asphalt shingles / sienna red
Eaves	Wood / dark brown paint

INTERIOR

Living room

Walls	Plaster / ivory paint
Floor	Oak / natural stain
Ceiling	Plaster / ivory paint
Trim	Oak / natural stain
Fireplace	Brick / unpainted
French doors	Oak / natural stain

Dining room

Walls	Mahogany paneling
Floor	Oak / natural stain
Ceiling	Plaster / ivory paint
Trim	Mahogany / natural stain
French door	Oak / mahogany veneer

Sunroom

Floor	Oak / natural stain
Walls	Plaster / ivory paint
Trim	Birch / natural stain
French doors	Oak / birch veneer

Bathroom

Walls	Ceramic / rectangular white tile
Floor	Porcelain / hexagonal white tile
Fixtures	Cast-iron enamel

CHESTER HOUSE
EXTERIOR

Siding	Porch	Pebble stucco / golden beige paint
	House	Clapboard / golden beige paint
Trim		Wood / white paint
Roof		Asphalt shingles / dark gray
Eaves		Wood / deep forest green paint

INTERIOR

Living room

Walls	Plaster / ivory paint
Trim	Mahogany / natural stain
Floor	Pine / natural stain
Ceiling	Mahogany beam / natural stain on plaster-painted ivory
Fireplace	Brick / light ivory paint

Dining room

Walls	Plaster / ivory paint
Trim	Mahogany / natural stain
Floor	Heart pine / natural stain
Ceiling	Fiberboard panels / natural white

Kitchen

Floor	Heart pine / natural stain
Walls	Plaster / natural white enamel paint
Trim	Oak / natural white paint
Cabinets	Pine / light yellow enamel paint
Counters	Corian / white

Bedroom

Floor	Pine / natural stain
Walls	Plaster / light yellow paint
Ceiling	Plaster / natural white
Trim	Pine / natural white

Bathroom

Floor	Porcelain hexagonal tiles / white and black
Walls	Pine-paneled wainscoting / white enamel paint
Fixtures	Standard

R E S O U R C E S

RUGS AND TEXTILES

■ ■

Arts & Crafts Period Textiles
5427 Telegraph Avenue, Suite W2H
Oakland, CA 94609
510/654-1645

Blue Hills Studios
  (floor treatments)
400 Woodland Way
Greenville, SC 29607
864/232-4217

Burrows Studio
J.R. Burrows & Company
PO Box 522
Rockland, MA 02370
800/347-1795
http://www.burrows.com

JAX Rugs
109 Parkway
Berea, KY 40403
606/986-5410

Nature's Loom
32 E. 31st Street
New York, NY 10016
800/365-2002

The Persian Carpet
5634 Chapel Hill Boulevard
Durham, NC 27707
800/333-1801

Prairie Textiles
Box 16567
St. Paul, MN 55116
612/228-9611
Catalog

Charles Rupert Designs
The Shop
2004 Oak Bay Avenue
Victoria, BC, Canada V8R 1E4
250/592-4916

Textile Artifacts
PO Box 501
Manhattan Beach, CA 90267
310/676-2424

FURNITURE AND HARDWARE

■ ■

Arts & Crafts Hardware
3860 Ellamae
Oakland, MI 48363
248/652-7652

Arts & Craftsman
43 East Tenth Street
New York, NY 10003
201/894-8140

Bakers
2240 Avalon Drive
Dayton, OH 45409
800/382-9663

Craftsman Hardware Co.
PO Box 161
Marceline, MO 64658
660/376-2481
Fax 660/376-4076

Crownpoint Cabinetry
153 Charlestown Road
PO Box 1560
Claremont, NH 03743
800/999-4994
http://www.crown-point.com

Ethan Allen
Ethan Allen Drive
Danbury, CT 06810
203/743-8000

Fairhaven Woodworks Co.
500 Larrabee Avenue
Bellingham, WA 98225
360/733-3411
tedscher@pacificrim.net
www.pacificrim.net/~tedschere

Scott Jordan Furniture
137 Varick Street (at Spring)
New York, NY 10013
212/620-4682

Warren Hile Studio, Inc.
89 East Montecito Avenue
Sierra Madre, CA 91024
626/355-4382
HileStudio@aol.com

Holton Furniture and Frame
5515 Doyle Street, #2
Emeryville, CA 94608
800/250-5277

Paul Kemner, Furniture Craftsman
2829 Rockwood
Toledo, OH 43610
419/241-8278

Kennebec Company (kitchens)
One Front Street
Bath, ME 04530
207/443-2131

MT Maxwell Furniture Co.
715 Liberty Street
Bedford, VA 24523
800/686-1844
MTMaxwell@aol.com

Sawbridge Studios
406 North Clark Street
Chicago, IL 60610
312/828-0055

L. and J.G. Stickley, Inc.
Stickley Drive, PO Box 480
Manlius, NY 13104
315/682-5500
Catalog

Trebuchet Workshop
613 Village Street
Kalamazoo, MI 49008
616/384-0183
TrebuchetW@aol.com

LAMPS AND LIGHTING FIXTURES
■ ■

Arroyo Craftsman
4509 Little John Street
Baldwin Park, CA 91706
818/960-9411

Louis Glesmann
240 S.E. Second Avenue
Delray Beach, FL 33444
561/274-3950

Metro Lighting
2216 San Pablo Avenue
Berkeley, CA 94702
888/638-7620

Mission Spirit
9900 West Spirit Lake Road
Spirit Lake, ID 83869
800/433-4211

Rejuvenation Lamp & Fixture Co
1100 S. E. Grand Avenue
Portland, OR 97214
503/231-1900

V. Michael Ashford
6543 Alpine Drive, SW
Olympia, WA 98512
360/352-0694
Catalog

Aurora Studios
109 Main Street
Putnam, CT 06260
800/448-7828
Catalog

Century Craftsman
PO Box 136, RR#1
Corbeil, ON, Canada P0H 1K0
705/752-2296
http://www.centurycraftsman.com

FMG Design
2601 West Farwell
Chicago, IL 60645
773/761-2957

Historic Lighting
114 East Lemon Avenue
Monrovia, CA 91016
626/303/4899

Inspiration
Dennis Bertucci
RD 3 Box 451
Walton, NY 13856
607/865-8372

Mica Lamp Co.
517 State Street
Glendale, CA 91203
818/241-7227

ANTIQUE DEALERS
■ ■

Art & Design Twenty
115 East Union Street
Pasadena, CA 91103
626/395-7600

Arts & Crafts Emporium
434 North La Brea Avenue
Los Angeles, CA 90036
213/935-3777

ASG Antiques
Ann & Leo Gallarano
Rt 2 Box 66
Berkeley Springs, WV 25411
304/258-4037

Blackwelders
696 East Colorado Boulevard
Pasadena CA 91101
626/584-0723

Butterfield & Butterfield
   (auctioneers and appraisers)
220 San Bruno Avenue
San Francisco, CA 94103
415/861-7500

Cathers & Dembrosky
43 East Tenth Street
New York, NY 10003
201/894-8140

Circa 87 -
   Antique & Artisan Center
69 Jefferson Street
Stamford, CT 06902
203/968-6485
circa87@aol.com

Craftsman Auctions
109 Main Street
Putnam, CT 06260
800/448-7828

Craftsman Style
1453 Fourth Street
Santa Monica, CA 90401
310/393-1468

Dalton's Antiques
1931 James Street
Syracuse, NY 13206
315/463-1568

Geoffrey Diner Gallery
1730 21st Street NW
Washington, DC 20009
202/483-5005
Fax 202/483-5005

Michael Fitzsimmons
   Decorative Arts
311 West Superior Street
Chicago, IL 60610
312/787-0496

Gallery 532 in Manhattan
142 Duane Street
New York, NY 10013
212/219-1327

JMW Gallery
144 Lincoln Street
Boston, MA 02111
617/338-9097

Mayfield Antiques
445 Bridge Street
Grand Rapids, MI 49504
616/451-3430

Mission Possible
5516 Connecticut Avenue, NW
Washington, DC 20015
202/363-6897

Peter-Roberts Antiques, Inc.
134 Spring Street
New York, NY 10012
212/226-4777

Phil Taylor Antiques
2007 N. Court Street
Ottumwa, IA 52501
515/682-7492

John Toomey Gallery
818 North Boulevard
Oak Park, IL 60301
708/383-5234

Voorhees Craftsman
Steve and Mary Ann Voorhees
1736 Lombard Street
San Francisco, CA 94123
707/584-5044

ART, GLASS, METAL AND GRAPHIC DESIGNERS
■ ■

Aurora Silversmith
PO Box 140
East Aurora, NY 14052
716/652-6043

FMG Design (metalwork)
2601 West Farwell
Chicago, IL 60645
773/761-2957

Fair Oak Workshops
PO Box 5578
River Forest, IL 60305
800/341-0597

Raymond Groll
P.O. Box 421, Station A
Flushing, NY 11358
718/463-0059

The Heintz Art Metal Shop
David H. Surgan
328 Flatbush Avenue, Suite 123
Brooklyn, NY 11238
718/638-3768

Historical Arts & Casting, Inc.
5580 W. Bagley Park Road
West Jordan, UT 84088
801/280-2400
800/225-1414

Judson Studios
Stained & Faceted Glass
200 South Avenue 66
Los Angeles, CA 90042
213/255-0131
800/445-8376

Roycroft China - Roycroft Shops
31 South Grove Street
East Aurora, NY 14052
716/652-333

Roycroft Potters
37 South Grove Street
East Aurora, NY 14052
716/652-7422

Stickley Brothers Copper
880 Foxcreek Lane
Cincinnati, OH 45233
513/941-9689

Steven Thomas, Inc. (art)
Box 41
Woodstock, VT 05091
802/457-1764

United Crafts
127 West Putnam Avenue
Greenwich, CT 06830
203/869-4898

PAINTS, TILES AND WALLPAPER
■■

Bradbury & Bradbury
PO Box 155
Benicia, CA 94510
707/746-1900

Helen Foster Stencils
71 Main Street
Sanford, ME 04073
207/490-2625

Historic Colors of America
Color Guild International
3090 S. Jamaica Court, Suite 100
Aurora, CO 80014
800/995-8885

Carol Mead Design
434 Deerfield Road
Pomfret Center, CT 06259
860/963-1927

Motawi Tileworks
33 N. Staebler, Suite 2
Ann Arbor, MI 48103
734/213-0017

Olde Century Colors
Primrose Distributing
54445 Rose Road
South Bend, IN 46628
800/222-3092

Charles Rupert
The Shop (William Morris
    wallpapers and fabrics)
2004 Oak Bay Avenue
Victoria, BC, Canada V8R 1E4
250/592-4916

Ann Sacks Tile and Stone
1210 SE Grand
Portland, OR 97214
503/233-0611
Catalog

Sanderson
(Morris & Co. Collection)
979 Third Avenue
New York, NY 10022
212/319-7220

The Stencil Collector
1723 Tilghman Street
Allentown, PA 18104
610/433-2105

Stencil World
530 Main Street, Suite 871
New Rochele, NY 10801
800/274-7997

Tile Restoration Center, Inc
3511 Interlake North, Dept PG
Seattle, WA 98103
206/633-4866

CHINA, POTTERY and GIFTS
■■

Ephraim Faience Pottery
PO Box 792
Brookfield, WI 53008
888/704-7687
608/764-1302

Gamble House Bookstore
4 Westmoreland Place
Pasadena, CA 91103
626/449-4178

Grovewood Gallery
111 Grovewood Road
Asheville, NC 28804
704/253-7651

O'Very/Covey Fine Papers
682 South 700 East
Salt Lake City, UT 84102
800/340-6063
Catalog

The Roycrofts Shops
31 South Grove Street
East Aurora, NY 14052
716/652-3333

INTERIOR DESIGNERS and ARCHITECTS
■■

Matthew Bialecki Associates
108 Main Street
New Paltz, NY 12561
914/255-6131
Fax 914/255-6276

Interior Vision
Karen L. Hovde
23 Oak Shore Court
Port Townsend, WA 98368
360/385-3161

Gerald Lee Morosco Architects, PC
50 South 15th Street
Pittsburgh, PA 15203
412/431-4347

O'Leary Cole, Inc
1320 E. North Street
Greenville, SC 29607
Builder/Designer
864/233-1606

Todd Schwebel Gallery
312/280-1998

MAGAZINES, JOURNALS, INFORMATION SOURCES
■■

American Bungalow
123 South Baldwin Avenue
PO Box 756
Sierra Madre, CA 91025
626/355-3363
www.ambungalow.com

Arts & Crafts Press
PO Box 5217
Berkeley, CA 94705
510/849-2117

Craftsman Farms
   (originally owned by
   Gustav Stickley)
Morris, NJ
973/540-1165

Craftsman Homeowner Magazine
31 South Grove Street
East Aurora, NY 14052
716/652-3333

Frank Lloyd Wright Home and
Studio
Museum Shop
951 Chicago Avenue
Oak Park, IL 60302
708/848-1976

Grove Park Inn Arts and Crafts
Conference
(3rd weekend of February)
Asheville, NC
800/438-5800
704/254-1912

Old House Interiors
2 Main Street
Gloucester, MA 01930
978/283-3200

Old House Journal
2 Main Street
Gloucester, MA 01930
978/283-3200

Style 1900
333 North Main Street
Lambertville, NJ 08530
609/397-4104
style1900@aol.com